THE GIRL IN THE MIRROR

THE GIRL IN THE MIRROR

Book One

SHEILA BROOKS

THE GIRL IN THE MIRROR
BOOK ONE

iUniverse books may be ordered through booksellers or by contacting:

iUniverse
1663 Liberty Drive
Bloomington, IN 47403
www.iuniverse.com
1-800-Authors (1-800-288-4677)

ISBN: 978-1-4917-4464-2 (sc)
ISBN: 978-1-4917-4463-5 (e)

Library of Congress Control Number: 2014915448

Printed in the United States of America.

iUniverse rev. date: 10/21/2014

PREFACE

It's not a coincidence that I'm here right now, in this place. It's almost as if I saw it coming. I did not know the details, but I certainly can say, I know that challenges or should I say more challenges were ahead of me. What I've learned is when you make a decision to pursue something, let's say a dream or career, or decide to be in a relationship, you are also making a decision to endure hardships and work through obstacles. What happens when things don't go quite the way you expected them to or when you feel that you endured the hardships and worked through obstacles or trying to anyway and things still seem to not work out for the best?

I lay in the bed remembering how it started with us. In spite of my reasoning to not go to dating sites to meet men, I did. I knew in my heart that was what I was supposed to do. After talking to a few guys, who were not appealing to me at all, I met him. In fact, I had decided to not talk to any more people from the site because I felt that it was a waste of my time. That's when it happened.

I got a message from him and I sent him my telephone number to call me. At this point, I did not want to go through all of the shenanigans of emailing messages back and forth. I felt that I could get a better feel of him if I talked directly to him. At the same time I was rather nonchalant about the whole meeting. He sent me a message asking me how about we go out this weekend and I said that sounds like a plan and I gave him my telephone number.

Sometimes in life we do things that feel right. We go along with things that we know that we are supposed to do or not supposed to do. Either way we do them at a cost. The roads that lie ahead are not necessarily easy but if you pay attention, learn the lessons that are to be learned, and let your experiences make you wiser and better, it will ultimately pay off. That does not mean that it will be easy but well worth the work. That's what I, Sheila learned throughout the years.

CHAPTER 1

Hi, my name is Sheila and I was quite the little girl growing up. Many people were around, yet I felt so lonely. I loved my Granny Brooks. Granny Brooks was a catalyst in my life. She was the person who really took care of me. Granny Brooks was a member of McGuire Temple Church. I attended church with Granny Brooks on Sundays and for special services during the week. I loved going to church with Granny Brooks and became mentally and vaguely spiritually aware of God because of Granny Brooks.

Although Granny Brooks loved, cared for and nurtured me, she reprimanded me well when I misbehaved. Granny Brooks would spank me with a strap. She did not abuse me but when I needed to be put back in line, she did a good job of getting me back there. I always felt like I really needed that.

My mom Donna and I lived with her parents, Granny and Grandpa Brooks in a one bedroom apartment. Granny and Grandpa Brooks had nine children, four males and five females. My mom was child number six.

After my mom gave birth to me, she raised me in her parent's apartment where two of her younger siblings lived also. The apartment where we lived was in a six flat family owned building with three apartments on each side. Granny and Grandpa Brooks apartment was on the first floor along with Granny Brooks sister and her husbands who lived next door. I played in the backyard a lot, especially during the summer months. Sometimes my cousins would visit and I would have someone to play with.

Granny Brooks took care of me. In fact, Granny Brooks nurtured and cared for me more than my own mother did. My mom did her best with me but Granny Brooks helped me grow and develop in ways my mom could not. I am sure this had a lot to do with the fact that my mom was only sixteen years old when she gave birth to me.

One day I was playing in the back yard when my Uncle George came in the backyard through the alley along with his friend that lived across the alley. Uncle George went in the house and his friend took me out of the back yard and to the outside basement of his building, right across the alley. He pulled my panties to the side while holding me in his arms and slightly penetrated me. I was confused and did not know or understand what was going on. After all, I was only six years old. I actually kind of enjoyed what he was doing. Yet I was confused.

Sometimes when children are sexually taken advantage of by adults or teenagers, the perpetrator does not necessarily hurt the child and the child may actually like how it feels. This can lead to mixed messages and the child can develop an unhealthy attitude towards sex and themselves. A child may feel that something is wrong with them for enjoying the sexual act that should not be happening. These sexual encounters that children experience at the hands of adults, many times will cause a child to become promiscuous, having enjoyed the experience and continuing to seek similar experiences to receive the same pleasure. The child may feel really guilty and ashamed about their behavior, yet a cycle has been set in motion.

I experienced several other similar incidents with different men over the years as a minor child. For each experience, I enjoyed what was being done to me and welcomed it, although those grown men had no business interacting with me in this sexual way. I enjoyed these experiences until my mother's boyfriend Carl fondled me when I was twelve years old.

As a child you expect the adults and caregivers in your life to love and protect you. When they violate your innocence and fail to nurture you in the appropriate way, you become confused. How can someone that is here to care for me do things to hurt me in this way? That is what I wondered. I attempted to tell my mother on several occasions but she didn't believe me or she just ignored me so that she would not have to confront her boyfriend and risk losing him. My mom made it okay for Carl to continue to violate me in sexual ways. Not only was I violated sexually but I suffered emotionally as well.

Children who are sexually molested often have no one to turn to. They are usually afraid to tell someone about the abuse and God forbid if they do tell and they are ignored, not believed or told that they are lying or worse, told that they are crazy. I believe that some children do not tell their mother in particular because they fear that their mother will not believe them anyway. That is a really tough spot to be in, especially as a child, who's only job should be is to be a child.

CHAPTER 2

Throughout the earlier part of grade school my mom married a man named Thomas. Thomas's parents were really good to me. They would care for me most of the time. Thomas's father Thomas Sr. loved to cook. He cooked for his household and he cooked for me too. I loved his cooking. He pretty much included me as part of his household since I was always with him.

Thomas Jrs. parents, Mr. and Mrs. McGuire lived on the second floor of a two flat that they owned, along with their daughter Keyshia. Keyshia was eight years younger than Thomas Jr. Thomas Jr., my mom, and I occupied the first floor of the two flat building. When Thomas III came along he joined us.

Mrs. McGuire had a section in the basement of the building as a dance studio. The other section of the building was a recording studio. I was part of the dance class that Mrs. McGuire taught. Thomas Jr. had a band and they would often rehearse in the studio.

Before Mrs. McGuire had part of the basement constructed into a dance studio, she held classes at the Day Care Center that she worked at. Dance classes were on Saturday mornings. Every year in June, we put on a really big show at Doones High School. We were also invited to perform at another dance class show every year.

Dance class was good for me. It gave me something productive to do on Saturday mornings. It also kept me out of my mother's hair. After dance class, I would go to Granny Brooks house and spend the night. Granny Brooks was the hair presser of the family and she would press my hair on some Saturdays, when my mom washed it.

Other family members came to visit Granny Brooks every Saturday afternoon. Sometimes she would press my Aunt Linda's hair too. Granny Brooks would have the radio on an AM Gospel station towards Saturday evening. I attended church with Granny Brooks every Sunday morning and stayed at church with her all day until someone took me home.

Having been a regular church attendee with Granny Brooks, I had a concept of God. I knew there was a God, although at the time I did not really know what that meant. Even though that was the case, I can honestly say that I always felt connected to God but I did not have a good cognitive understanding about what I was experiencing. I knew God was there and that he comforted me. I could feel his presence at a very early age.

Elder Saga was the pastor of Saga Temple Church. Elder Saga was a really cool pastor. He kept peppermint candy in his pocket and would give them away to us children as a token of his love. We loved the peppermint candy and would often ask him for some. We really thought we had a treat when Elder Saga gave us the peppermint candy and I guess we did, coming from a man with so much love. Elder Saga and Granny Brooks were really good friends and if you did not know any better, you would have thought that they were an item. Elder Saga did have a wife that is until she passed away.

Sundays were a special time for me too. I had some really cool friends at church. After Sunday school a group of us children would walk to the store to by snacks. It was quite the ritual. I was also in the choir. I don't remember asking to be in the choir or even being asked if I wanted to be. I was put in there by my Granny Brooks of course, but it was cool and good for me.

CHAPTER 3

Most times when dance class was over, I would go to Granny Brooks house. As I grew older, I stopped attending dance class and I did not go to Granny Brooks house as much on the weekend. The church bus was up and running and I was sent to church while my mother stayed home. I could not understand why I was sent to church rather than go to church with my mom.

After my brother Thomas III was born, I had a sibling to care for. Having a baby brother was fun for me. Aside from church it gave me something to look forward to. School was okay for me too. It gave me another outlet. I was quiet for the most part and I was happy about being at school most of the time.

One day when I was in the fourth grade, I was at school and I observed a group of girls picking on a girl in my class named Lashawn. Lashawn was a nice, quiet girl. I thought, "why in the world would anyone want to bother Lashawn". One particular girl in the bully group threatened that she would beat Lashawn up after school. After school the group of bully girls approached Lashawn and the next thing I knew, Lashawn had the hair of the girl that threatened her and she was swinging her around in a circle by her head.

When Lashawn released her hair, all the bully girls ran away. Watching that taught me that just because someone is quiet and nice does not mean that they won't defend themselves if they need to. I would learn throughout life that people will definitely target you if you are quiet and nice. Unfortunately, many people see that as being weak. The question that resonated in my mind was "why would someone want to hurt someone else because they are weak?". Shouldn't we help the weak? I had a long journey in front of me and would frequently observe many individuals preying on the weak.

My Aunt Stacia had a boyfriend that lived across the street. She would frequently visit us so she could go over to her boyfriend Charlie's house. Charlie had four brothers, Charlie being the oldest. They lived in an apartment with their mother. One day I was sitting on the front porch when Charlie's 20 year old brother Rodney came over. He suggested that I come with him and so I did.

Rodney took me inside of their apartment. He eventually took me into a really big hallway closet and laid me on the floor. He began to fondle me as I lie there with my eyes closed. Rodney kept getting up and leaving out of the closet. He would return and continue fondling me. He had been checking the scene to make sure no one was coming. When he had enough he let me out of the closet and out of the front door. I went home as if everything was normal. These kinds of incidents were becoming normal for me.

CHAPTER 4

My mom had started seeing another man while she was still married to Thomas Jr. She spent less time at home and more time with her new love interest. This meant that she spent little or no time with me. Thomas Sr. looked after me most of the time. When I came home from school I would be with Thomas Sr. He fed me and made sure I was taken care of. Eventually, my mom had taken me with her to live with her new boyfriend, Tony. I was definitely saddened that I would not spend time with Thomas Sr.. After all, Thomas Sr. took really good care of me and he was really fun too!

My mom, Tony, Thomas III and I lived in a one bedroom apartment on the first floor of a four unit apartment building. Tony's mom and step dad lived next door. Tony's two older sons also lived next door. I made friends with a girl that lived on the second floor on the other side from our apartment. Her name was Crystal. I would visit Crystal from time to time. Crystal lived wither mom and dad. They were nice people. They both worked and Crystal had nice things to show for it. Crystal and I enjoyed hanging out together. Crystal and her family moved after about a year after we moved there.

I also met some people in the neighborhood. Across the street lived a really huge family in a two flat building. They were the Williams and they occupied both the first floor, second floor and basement of the building. There was a girl named Blue who was a couple of years older than me. We become really good friends. Blue had a younger sister named Tomeka who was my age but Blue and I hit it off so good that we were better friends than Tomeka and I. I was really fascinated with Blue. She had a way about herself that appealed to me.

My mom frequently sent me to the grocery store to get groceries. The grocery store was quite a little ways. Most of the time, the list for the grocery store was quite a bit for a little girl to carry on her own, so I would always ask a friend to accompany me. I went to ask Blue to go to the store with me most of the time and would have to wait for her to get dressed and sometimes to wait on her to do whatever else it was that she had to do. I would wait, sometimes for hours. I know sometimes she would stall just so I could just leave because she was taking too long, and then she wouldn't have to go because the truth is she didn't want to go and I don't blame her. After a while it just got to be a little bit too much.

My moma would sometimes be angry with me that it took me so long to go to the store and get back home. I just dealt with the reprimand because I needed people to help me with the groceries. I thought so, anyway. Then again, maybe I just didn't want to go by myself. I was sure that many times Blue didn't want to go to the store with me, but she never said no.

I summoned some other friends in the neighborhood to go to the store with me to give Blue a break. They were mainly friends I knew from school. Those friends would procrastinate and take their time too instead of saying no. I kind of appreciated them going in spite of the fact that they really didn't want to go. I did not want to get on their nerves either and so eventually I started making some attempts to go to the grocery store on my own. When I knew that the groceries would be too heavy for me alone I would ask one of my store friends to go with me.

Crystal and her parents moved and I was kind of sad. I missed visiting Crystal. Soon after, a new family moved on the second floor above our apartment. There was a lady, her boyfriend, and two girls. The oldest girl was my age and the other girl was three years younger than us. The oldest girls name was Sandy and the youngest girls name was Ivy. We would walk to school together and wait on each other after school and walk home together. Then one day Sandy and Ivy were not coming out and I was running so I left and walked to school without them.

After school Sandy approached me wanting to fight, saying that I did not pick her up for school. I just walked away from her. My thoughts were, *you live upstairs from me and you have to come down past me to get out of the door and you're angry because I didn't pick you up from school, and I do not have to, it's not a rule.* At a very young age, I would reason. I would try to make some sense of some things that I experienced. What people did and what they said. What I believed so far was that people do and say things that either make no sense or just shouldn't be, like grown men messing with little girls, or boys.

CHAPTER 5

I had become accustomed to being the care taker of the home. I did the cleaning, went to the laundromat to wash the clothes, sheets and towels, did the grocery shopping and cared for my little brother. When my youngest little brother came, I cared for him too. That makes two little boys that I was caring for. My mom and Tony worked. Those were the roles that everyone played in the household.

I had a friend at school named Lakita. Lakita told me about a party that one of the girls at our school was having that Friday night. I really wanted to go. I never got a chance to do anything fun. Not with my friends anyway. I asked my mother if I could go to the party and she said we'll see. When Friday came my mom sent me to the Laundromat and when I returned home, I asked my mom if I could go to the party. My mom did not answer me at first. I waited a while and asked her again and she said no.

I had had enough of not being able to be a kid. I left out of the house and went to Lakita's house. After a while, we went to the party together. The party was definitely a different environment than what I was used to. After all, I didn't get to go to parties or anything considered fun for that matter. I made the best out of my time out. It had gotten really late and I decided against going back home. I ended up spending the night at the house where the party was. The girl whose party it was name was Angela.

I did not know how I ended up spending the night at Angela's house. I assumed that Lakita said something to Angela and Angela told her parents and they said it was okay for me to spend the night. The weird thing is that I did not say anything to Lakita, so how did she say something to Angela? *Sometimes others can sense when children are not happy at home.*

The next morning I saw Angela's parents and they spoke to me. I spoke back. They never asked me any questions. I got the feeling that they were asking Angela all of the questions. They never really acted like they didn't want me there but I felt that they were not all that comfortable with me continuing to be there. After all, no one spoke to my parents to see if it was okay for me to spend the night there, and I was a minor. Again, I knew her parents knew that something was not right at my home and they felt for me but were in a really awkward position.

I understood and decided to make a move. The only thing was that I definitely did not want to go home. I was trying to escape that place at all cost so I called Granny Brooks. Granny Brooks had my aunt Stacia come to get me. I ended up spending the remainder of the weekend at Granny Brooks house but I was back home on Sunday evening after church.

Life sucked as a kid for me but I did my best to make the best of it. Tony's daughter came to visit for a long while. Her name was Katie. Katie was in her early twenties. She was nice to me and acted like a big sister to me. It was fun to have her as a big sister. My mom would let me go with Katie from time to time. Katie did not mind at all. We went to the movies, the mall, and some other fun places. I had a lot of fun with Katie and that was the most fun I had as a kid thus far.

Katie was an angel that God sent especially for me, to ease my pain and give me some happy times. I was sure sad to see her leave. I knew that the fun was over. Although Katie was gone, I was determined to be a kid and have fun. I guess some would say that I became rebellious, but I felt at the time that I am going to be a kid rather my mom and her boyfriend liked it or not. Later in life, I learned that what I was doing even as a child was taking my power back. How fascinating it is for a child to have to take their power back from their parents who are trying to take their childhood from them, and make them into a prisoner. That's how I felt anyway, like a prisoner, except for when Katie was there.

CHAPTER 6

When I was in eighth grade we moved to another apartment on the southeast side of Chicago. We lived on the second floor of a two flat. On the first floor was a family with a mother, father and two girls. The oldest girl was a couple of years older than me. Her name was Joanie and her little sister's name was Diamond.

At first I had a little bit of a hard time at my new school. There was a boy and he wanted to show off for his girlfriend by making fun of me. That's what he did. Everyone would just look and so did I. I did not feel a need to respond. I thought it was stupid. I did not like it of course, and it was a little scary for me but I still thought they were both stupid, him for being ignorant and his girlfriend for laughing and thinking it was cute.

Other than that initial nonsense, the remainder of eighth grade went okay for me. I had a couple of goofy incidents, one in which a girl I sat by in class dared me to light up a cigarette that she had and I did. I was sent to the office. The principle reprimanded me and they called my mom to come and pick me up. We had a substitute teacher that day and I thought I was off the hook with my homeroom teacher but she found out. I could tell by the way she looked at me the next day in school. She didn't like me anyway so it didn't really matter.

The other goofy incident was when I got out of line because the teacher told me to go to the end of the line. Instead of going to the end of the line, I went straight down the stairs and into the office. I explained how another student, Joe was looking at me and making goofy faces and smiling at me, and all I was doing was looking at him and the teacher told me to go to the end of the line. I think she just wanted to get to me for when I lit up the cigarette. She was not there and the situation had been tended to so she had nothing to punish me for. It seems that she just wanted me to be punished by her.

After graduating from grammar school, I went to High School. High School was pretty cool for the most part. In my freshmen year I called myself dating a guy named Coolio. Coolio was short and dark. Since I was dealing with craziness at home, it was no surprise that I did not come home from school one day. Instead, I went home with Coolio. Coolio lived with a woman that he called moma. She was not his real moma though, and I am not sure how he had come to know her and furthermore call her moma. She had a daughter and a son, whom Coolio called his sister and brother.

I spent the night and I slept in the room with the girl that Coolio called his sister. I am not sure what Coolio told "his moma" to allow me to stay and spend the night. The next morning we went to a house that he said was his aunt's house. There was a lady that was always there named Niko. Niko was nice and she allowed us to hang out there. Coolio called Niko his cousin. Since I did not go to school that day or the next couple of days, I needed a note to go back to school. Coolio asked Niko to write me a note and sign my mother's name and she did.

I eventually went back home and faced the punishment that I never seemed to escape. I was always on punishment which was a lot of the reason that I just did what I wanted to do without regard or consideration for my mom or her boyfriend. I was determined to be a child and in many ways be free, for a little while anyway.

Throughout high school I had a few boyfriends that went to South Shore Community High School. I also had a boyfriend who did not go to South Shore Community High School. I had a good friend named Trina, whom I knew from my old neighborhood. We stayed in contact and talked just about every day, every weekday anyway. I could only talk on the weekdays when my mom and her boyfriend were at work. The weekends were out for talking on the telephone.

I loved New Edition, a singing group of young boys, teenagers at the time. Trina knew a boy that used to live in her neighborhood at the time, that she said looked like, acted like and sang like one of the boys from New Edition. She told me about him and asked if she could give him my telephone number. I agreed and he called me. His name was Jodie. Jodie sure did sing like Ralph Tresvant from New Edition. He thought so anyway. He also tried to imitate his style and wore his hair in a low cut with hair hanging at the nape of his neck, just like Ralph Tresvant. I called it a shag.

Jodie and I became really tight. We talked on the telephone all the time and we visited each other regularly. All of this was hidden from my mom and her boyfriend, of course. When school was out in the summer, Jodie would come to my house while my mom and Tony were at work and when school was in, either I would cut school sometimes and he would come over or I would go to his house when I got out of school. Sometimes on the weekend, I would find a way to escape and go to his house on the weekend. For a short period of time I did not go see Jodie as much because I had joined the track team, so I would practice on the days of track practice and sometimes when I didn't have track practice, I would go to his house. At one point during my southmore year, I had another boyfriend that went to my school also.

One day a boy in my history class told me I looked just like his girlfriend. I asked him what was his girlfriends name and he said Janelle. I asked him if her name was Janelle Brooks and he said yes. "That is my cousin", I said. That guy also was good friends with the boyfriend that I had at my high school.

One day I was walking with Jodie, his friend, and a friend of mine. We were headed in the direction of my house, when a car pulled up beside us. I looked in the car and saw my cousin Janelle and her boyfriend, the boy in my history class. I just took off running. I ended up telling on myself. I told Jodie about my boyfriend at school. I felt busted and so I had to explain my behavior. My friend went home and so did I.

After a while I came out of my house and there Jodie was sitting on my stairs drinking liquor. He was crying and his friend was trying to console him and was saying to him, "man, let's go". I told Jodie that he had to leave and eventually they left. I realized later that I did not have to even tell on myself. I could have just went along with it but I believe that the reason I responded that way was because I thought that my cousins boyfriend was getting ready to bust me out, especially considering the way he pulled up like, yeah you're busted, and so I thought I was.

I really did not think much about what happened. I did not understand why Jodie was so hurt. I guess I was not yet in touch with the sensitivities and feelings of another, particularly in a situation like that. I knew that boys hurt girls but I had no idea that a girl could hurt a boy. I am now reminded of Coolio and the fact that he followed me home from school one day crying, after I had broken up with him.

It was all weird to me but soon I learned what it was like to be hurt in that way. In fact, throughout the remainder of Jodie's and I relationship, all he did was inflict hurt and pain on me. He became a big time cheater. I guess that was his reaction to his hurt and I mean when I say it was a non stop, repetitive cylcle, it was no joke. Then me and my immaturity and vulnerability prevented me from removing myself from such unhealthy situations, which was yet to come.

CHAPTER 7

After having so much trouble at home and having an abortion, my persistence about being in a relationship with Jodie led to another pregnancy a year after I had an abortion. I was sixteen years old. Prior to me finding out that I was pregnant there was an incident that led me to leaving home and not returning there again until my late twenties.

One Friday night, Tony came home late and drunk. He came in my room and went to my dresser and put Vaseline on his fingers. He then came where I was in my bed and fondled my vagina. After a little bit, I got up and ran to the bathroom. He came to the bathroom door and asked me what was wrong. I never answered. I stayed in the bathroom for a long time until I knew he was gone. Eventually, I came out and got back in my bed. All that time, my mother was sleep.

The next morning, my mother came into my room to put some clothes up because she had been doing laundry. I had the incident that had happened the night before on my mind and I was confused and felt I could not continue to live like that. I must have been looking a certain kind of way because my mom asked me what was wrong with me. I told her to ask Tony. She must have went and asked Tony what was wrong with me because I heard him yelling, "I didn't do anything to her. I didn't touch her". The funny thing is that I never said he did anything to me, I only said, "ask Tony". Tony had pretty much told on himself and my mom knew it.

My mom told me she was going to talk to a lawyer and I said okay. Two weeks later she told me that for her to talk to a lawyer it would cost $200. I was dumbfounded because here I was a kid and I didn't need to be involved in how much it would cost. Then she said, "just forget about it". I guess she meant her talking to a lawyer, as well as what Tony had done to me.

As you can imagine, that did not sit well with me. In fact, it hurt me to the core. Here I was being told by my mother to disregard what her boyfriend did to me sexually and furthermore to forget about doing anything about it. I was devestated. I felt that as long as Tony knew that my mother would not do anything about what he was doing to me, he felt that he could continue to do whatever he wanted to with me. It wasn't enough that he had been physically, verbally, and emotionally abusive. Now my mom was making it clear to him that it was okay for him to be sexually abusive to me too!

I was not going for that. Soon after, I realized that I was pregnant again with Jodie's baby, of course. I was already determined that I was going to keep it. I was sixteen years old and going into my junior year in High School. I definitely did not want to continue to live with my mother and her boyfriend. I went to my Granny Brooks house and petitioned to her to let me live with her. I told her that I could no longer live with my mother. My Granny allowed me to stay with her for a few days but one day she took me back to my mother's house.

As we were walking up the stairs, we could see and hear Tony pacing back and forth saying, "she needs to apologize". He said it over and over again. My mother was pacing back and forth too, saying nothing and looking worried and confused. I realized that she was torn between doing right by me and the consequences of letting him go. Hearing him continuously say she needs to apologize (he was talking about me) and see her response crushed me, and I mean deep. The next thing I know is, I screamed at the top of my lungs, "I HATE YOU"! I ran down the stairs and out of the building. Eventually Granny Brooks came out too and we left.

I lived with my grandparents and in the Fall I gave birth to a baby girl. I was at Jodie's house on the toilet and I felt like I had to have a bow movement but something was not right. I was only 28 weeks which is about 7 months. I told Jodie that something was wrong, he told his mother and she called the ambulance. The paramedics took me to the hospital and soon after, Christiana Sheann Phillips was born. She was 2 pounds. Christina was under the weight for a newborn to come home. She had to stay in the hospital for 2 ½ months. I visited her regularly and sometimes Jodie came with me. Family members of both Jodie and I visited at least once.

Having Christina was a turning point in my life. Giving birth at the age of sixteen and being a new mother was all semi-surreal to me. I say this because I was so used to taking care of my brothers and other children that sometimes I felt like they were my children, but this was different. Christina was my baby for sure. I had to take care of her from birth. When Christina came home from the hospital, I had to tend to her every need. I had to feed her throughout the day and night. I had to change her pampers, bathe her, dress her, and be responsible for her being healthy and safe.

I warmed up to motherhood rather fast. Although I was a teenager, I did my best to be a good mother above everything else. I also had a lot of help with Christina. Granny Brooks cared for Christina so I could go to school or work, and other family members would want to keep her a lot, and so I allowed it most times. Soon after Christina came home from the hospital, I moved in with Jodie and his family. In their home was Jodie's mother, Phyllis, his brother, Trent, and Phyllis's boyfriend, Carl. They lived in a townhouse. At the time, I was receiving public assistance or what they called welfare. I was willing to pay rent and Phyllis took advantage of my willingness to pay rent, knowing I received public assistance.

Phyllis and Carl were also very much involved with drugs. Crack cocaine was their drug of choice. Crack cocaine drove them to expunge as much money out of me as they could. Along with that, Jodie liked to drink and fight. I would fight him back but after a while, I just got really tired of fighting.

Jodie worked at Popeyes chicken and he had a friend named Chuck who also worked at Popeyes. Chuck had a girlfriend named Benita and they had two children together. Jodie and I started hanging out with them and after a while I was staying at Benita's house. I met a couple of young ladies, Regina and Carol. They were really good friends who lived right across the street from one another. They both lived around the corner from Benita's house. I became good friends with Regina and Carol, Regina more than Carol.

Regina had a son who was not quite a year old yet. I hung out with them quite often and for a short time, Regina and I worked together at Soldier Field, the Chicago Bears Stadium. When we learned that they were hiring for people to work when the Bears had their games at home, we went and applied together. We both got hired along with a male friend of hers and we would go to work together and come home together too.

After being at Benita's house for a while, I knew that it was about time for me to leave. When Benita's grandmother passed away, she left her house to Benita, her mom and her uncle, who lived in the basement. This caused Benita to feel like she had some say in who could live there, and I guess I thought so too. The situation was starting to feel tense and I also started to feel like this was not how I was supposed to continue living.

One day Jodie and I had sex in a car that was stored in their garage and we fell asleep. The next morning, Benita's mother came out and saw us and told us that we needed to leave. I ended up leaving there and going back to Jodie's house. That did not go so great and it only lasted for a little while. I could not take the fighting and so one day I decided to leave. Phyllis pleaded with me to leave Christina there with her. I told her that she could stay for a little while but I would be coming back for her.

Around that time I had been hanging out with my friend Julia and her sister Angie. We would hang out at their older sister Nancy's house. Julia, Angie, and I were all about getting high. Our drug of choice was mainly crack cocaine which we would put on marijuana or cigarette tobacco in tobacco paper also known as tops. That only lasted for about four of five days because I could not take living like that either.

CHAPTER 8

I went and got Christina from Phyllis's and went back to Granny Brooks house. I pretty much stayed at Granny Brooks house permanently. After Jodie and I reconciled, I would spend the night at his house quite often. Jodie and his family had moved several times throughout the remainder of our relationship. Jodie also became a big time cheater. Later I came to believe that I may somewhat have had something to do with that. The time when I told on myself after my cousin and her boyfriend rode up on me, may have been a turning point for Jodie. I believe that Jodie was devastated and really hurt because after that he was always cheating. He would cheat, get caught, and still want me to stay with him. I guess I was somewhat naïve, so I would stay, until I had finally had enough.

I did not graduate with my High School class. I had missed a half credit for photography class when I was pregnant with Christina. I had photography for first period at 8 o'clock in the morning and I was going through morning sickness. I would have to get myself together and that delayed me and made me late for my first period photography class. I would make it to school just in time for second period.

The following school year I was a demo senior and did not pass to my senior year. I was a half credit shy to progress to my senior year. A friend of mine talked me into talking to the school's principal about allowing me to arrange photography for independent study, to make up the work that I missed. This would allow me to earn the half credit and graduate on time. The principal agreed to allow me to talk to the photography teacher about this and she agreed.

When it came time for the prom and graduation I became reluctant. Prom and graduation required spending money which I did not have, not enough to take care of all of the expenses anyway. When I left Granny Brooks house, I called myself being grown and I did not feel comfortable asking my Granny or other family members to help me. I just stopped going to school and I did not graduate with my graduating class.

The following school year my friend Julia was pregnant. She had not graduated either. She went to sign up at an alternative High School where you could go to school in the evening and earn the credits you needed to graduate. I went with her and ended up registering too. The staff that the registered me was looking at me a little confused because he said that I only needed a half a credit in English to graduate. I guess he couldn't understand how a half credit stopped me from graduating but it did. I never explained the situation. The alternative school did not require as many electives, gym or ROTC like regular High Schools did. This only required me to take one class but I initially registered for four classes, two classes on two nights a week and two classes on two other nights a week. I eventually dropped two classes that I did not need that were on the same days.

Julia ended up having her baby right before school started and never attended classes. I attended classes and went on to graduate that school year. The summer after I graduated, I went to Olive-Harvey College with my friend Regina. She was going to register. When we left the building, I was registered for classes too. I always thought it was interesting how I went with other people to register for school and ended up registering myself and completing the programs, and getting my diploma and degree. Regina did not continue with her classes either, the same as Julia. It is as if they really went and asked me to go with them, but it was really about me without them knowing it. I believe it was God divinely orchestrating the events.

College was going really good. My Aunt Stacia moved out of the apartment upstairs from my grandparents and moved into a house soon after she got married. I asked my Great Aunt Deidra if I could rent that apartment. I was receiving public assistance and receiving stipends from school. Aunt Deidra agreed and I moved upstairs into my first very own apartment.

Things were looking up for me. Family members helped me by giving me pieces of furniture. My Aunt Linda's boyfriend Zachery gave me his living room furniture, a couch and a love seat. That really helped me a great deal. Soon after that he brought Christina a bunk bed. The bunk bed was really nice. It was red with a full size mattress at the bottom and a twin size mattress at the top. He also bought a desk and chair to go with it. Zachery really looked out for Christina. He was like a god father to her and I appreciated his love, care and concern for my daughter.

Since I had my own apartment, I no longer spent night's at Jodie's house. He spent nights at my apartment instead. He stayed there for the most part, but he would still spend time at his mom's house. He would mainly go to his mom's house when we got into it. Jodie and I had the craziest relationship, I thought so anyway. I saw other people and so did he. In fact, he always got busted and he very may have been doing more than what I knew about. I on the other hand never got busted. One day Jodie told me that I was a cheater too, I just never got caught. He was right and maybe he needed to learn from me how to cheat better.

Jodie and I continued with that ridiculous relationship until one day I had had enough. I did not want to continue to live like that and so I told him that we were done. He did not take that well and he refused to let go. One day he came by and I acted like a crazy person running and screaming. I even ran out of the building running and screaming. I just wanted him to leave and he did. I thought that was the end of it until he called a week later. I asked him what did he want and he said that he thought I just needed some air for a little bit.

Jodie wanted to play around with other girls but he wanted to have me too. For quite a while, I felt that he could just go and do what he wanted to and be with whatever girls he wanted to be with but it seemed that he had to have me too. I guess that had to do with how generous I was. I shared what I had with him. In a sense I kind of took care of him. I made sure he had clothes, shoes, money, etc. I did it to help him along his way and to get on his feet but that never happened. I could see why he wanted to hold on to me. Not that that was the only reason why but I'm sure that it contributed to it.

Jodie and I were permanently separated after that. It was real after seven plus years I had finally managed to let him go and keep it that way. Jodie's mom would keep Christina and that was really the only interaction that I had with them. They did not always have a working telephone and so sometimes I was not able to check on Christina or communicate with them about bringing her home or me coming to get her. I did not like that at all and a few times I went to their house to get her and they were not home.

I remember one day in particular when I went to get her and no one was home. I got a really bad feeling in my gut and did not feel comfortable about them keeping her anymore. It was a long while before I allowed them to keep her again. After Phyllis pretty much begged me to keep her, I let her. Slowly, I began to allow Christina to go with her but not nearly as often as before.

CHAPTER 9

After I graduated from Olive-Harvey Community College, I went to Chicago State University. I had learned about how to take advantage of all of the grants available including work study, while I was at Olive-Harvey Community College. Work study is a grant that you have to work for. I did my work study in the Social Science Department the first year I had work study and the Student Affairs office the second year I had it. I did one year of work study at Chicago State University in the Admissions office.

There was a group of girls that I knew from High School that I began to hang out with while going to Olive-Harvey Community College. We would get together and get high. I continued to hang out with these girls while attending Chicago State University. After being at Chicago State University (CSU) for three semesters, I withdrew. My first year was good and it went downhill after that. I started getting F's and the school would have eventually suspended me so I decided to withdraw. I knew that I was not in a state of mind to continue at that time. I also knew that although I withdrew, I would return and complete the course work to earn a degree.

I worked jobs here and there and made an effort to keep myself busy doing something constructive. I did pretty good at this for the most part but there were periods where I did not work. I didn't stay at jobs very long. I would last months and even close to a year. The longest I had worked a job was at a Day Care Center where I worked at for a whole year. I was able to do that because my rent was not much. I had it good. I would go back on welfare when I was in between jobs. There were periods where I did not pay my rent at all and I would pay a lump sum of what I was delinquent in out of money that I would get from stipends from school grants.

I paid rent to my Granny Brooks sister, Aunt Deidra and then her daughter, Maggie when she passed away. I lived in a family building and paid rent to family and so I was able to get by with a lot. I am sure that Aunt Deidra and Maggie did not like it but they dealt with it. Aunt Diedra told me that I would have to find somewhere else to stay one day. I guess she had had enough. I convinced her that I was going to get a job and that I would have the money. That was during one of those periods that I was not working and not paying my rent. I continued in the same cycle for a while.

After a year or so, Aunt Deidra passed away and her daughter Maggie took over. I continued the same cycle but Maggie wouldn't bother me about not paying rent when I hadn't. I felt bad about it and I made efforts to pay something. After all my rent was only three hundred and seventy five dollars for a decent one bedroom apartment. At the time one bedroom apartments were five hundred dollars and up a month.

CHAPTER 10

I grew up with quite a few people at Saga Temple Church. I was really close to one girl, Stacey. Stacey and I were the best of friends out of all of my other peers at Saga Temple Church. Stacey was working at the White Hen Pantry convenient store. Her brother in law managed it. He was also an associate pastor at Saga Temple Church. Stacey's sister was the manager's wife and my cousin who was good friends with the manager's wife worked there too.

Stacey and I were hanging out quite a bit around that time. She told me that her manager/brother in law Henry was hiring for another sales clerk. I went to the store and applied for the job. Henry hired me and I started working at White Hen Pantry. The funny thing is that by the time I started working there, Stacey was no longer there. Here it was again. It is as if she was there just so I could find out about the job and get it.

I was dating a guy named Stevie at the time. When I met Stevie he told me that his name was John and that his mother owned her own company where he worked for her. After dealing with him for a while I began to notice that he was never at work and then one day while he was leaving my apartment he said, "oh yeah, you can call me Stevie". I asked him why and he told me that his real name was Stevie and he did not know that we would get that far.

As I said before, Stevie was never at work and one day he mentioned something about his mother's job. I noticed he said job when initially he said that she owned the company and if that were true, he would have said her company or business instead of saying her job. Along with the fact that he had given me a phony name in the beginning led me to realize that he was a phony all the way around. Nothing he told me seemed to be true. I felt taken advantage of and really did not feel good about the relationship anymore. The thing is that I could not just walk away. I cared for him and had developed a bond with him.

Stevie had a glass eye and he had asthma. I guess that was true. I did quite a bit of so called helping him. I started to realize that when it came time for us to do things, I was always the one footing the bill. I eventually told him that he needed to get a job. He claimed that he had been looking for a job and I shared my bus tokens with him in hopes that he would get a job.

One day he told me that he had an interview and on the day of the interview, he called me at work. I asked him how the interview went and he told me that he did not go. I hung up. Stevie called back and I told him that he needed to stop calling me because I was at work. He told me that I was acting like that because he was not saying what I wanted to hear. He was right. I told him we were done and I hung up.

A couple of days later, my friend and I were coming out of my building when a car pulled up and the man that was driving asked me if I was Stevie's girlfriend. I was hesitant and said I was. I then noticed his cousin in the passenger seat. He spoke to me and told me that Stevie had passed away. He went on to say that he had an asthma attack the day before and he didn't make it. I was in a state of shock. He went on to tell me that he would let me know the funeral arrangements if I gave him my telephone number. I gave it to him and he called me a couple days later to give me the wake and funeral information.

I found myself feeling guilty about the whole thing. Knowing that just a little more than a few days before, I told him that we were done. I kind of felt that maybe he felt he had nothing to live for and just gave up. After some time I could sense God telling me that it was okay and that it was not my fault but it was his choice to let go and there was nothing I could have done about it.

My Granny and my friend Sharon went to the funeral with me. Sharon also invited her mother. When it came time to walk around to view the body, I kept my hands over my eyes. I just could not look at him. Later, I was glad that I did not look at him dead in that casket because that is not the way I wanted to remember him.

After I had learned of Stevie's death and before his funeral, a young man had come into the White Hen Pantry store where I worked. He worked at the Post Office next door to White Hen Pantry. He just looked at me grinning. He continued to come in the store flirting with me and getting a good look at my toes every chance he could. Finally, one day he passed me his telephone number on a piece of paper. I put it in my pocket and kept working.

One day I was at home feeling a little restless and thought to myself, I am bored. I remembered the telephone number in my work smock pocket the guy from the Post Office gave me. I went and got it to call. His name was Larry. I dialed the number and he answered the telephone. I asked to speak to Larry and he said it was him. I told him to come over to my apartment and he did. Larry came ready to please and I was gamed.

After that Larry continued to pursue me and I kind of went along with it. He seemed cool for the most part. He was really giddy about me and that really make me feel good. He acted as if he had hit the jackpot and that made me feel like a jackpot. He also made an effort to do things for me. He offered to pick me up from work and take me home. He offered to buy me food at times too. That was big to me. I absolutely was not used to that. I was used to being the one to put out and take care of things, most of the time anyway. I guess you can say that he wooed me. The funny thing is that Woo became his nickname for me, not because he wooed me but because of an incident I told him about.

The story was about a cab driver who asked me what was my name and I told him Woo. He was an African man and he tried to talk to me while I rode in his cab. When I got out of the cab, he began calling out to me to get my attention. The thing was that he was calling out Woo and that was not my name. It was really funny. Ever since then, Larry called me Woo most of the time.

Larry and I started getting more and more serious. I can say that Larry was very serious about me. Initially, it flattered me but after a while I became concerned. Although I was concerned, I continued to stay in a relationship with him. He was not the easiest person to walk away from. In other words, he was not willing to let go so easily. I soon realized that I had a real live case on my hands.

CHAPTER 11

Christina and I were riding in Larry's car one day and he pulled over, got out of the car and went to a pay phone. He began yelling obscenities and then he hung up. He made another call and began yelling obscenities again. I got out of the car, opened the back door, got Christina out and proceeded to walk off. Larry came over to where we were and said "sorry, sorry, please get back in the car". After a few minutes of hesitation, I got back into the car.

I never said anything about what happened. I was just really in shock. Clearly, he was talking to a woman that he was involved with or had been involved with. Whatever the case may have been he was involved enough to be so upset about whatever was happening. He was in a rage and when he hung the phone up he slammed it multiple times and really hard. I realized then again that I had a serious situation on my hands. Even though I hesitated to get back in the car, I knew that if I didn't get in I would on some level receive what I had just experienced him doing. The fact of the matter is that I had my daughter with me and I wanted her as well as myself to be safe, without drama. Therefore, I got back in the car and we proceeded with the remainder of our endeavor.

Larry and I spent quite a bit of time together. Christina had gotten close to him. He was good to Christina and treated her like his own daughter. In fact, I believe he prided himself on being a father figure to a little girl who was not biologically his own. It worked out well and since Christina's biological father was not a stand up dad, it was good for Christina to have Larry in her life. Ever since I had broken up with Jodie for good, he became more and more of a distant father to Christina.

Many of the times Jodie's mom Phyllis would ask for him to get her. If Phyllis had not asked for her granddaughter I don't believe that Jodie would have even seen her at all. I may be wrong about this but that was the picture I got. Jodie came and got Christina less and less and they never kept a telephone on long enough for Phyllis and I to communicate concerning her getting Christina. We (Phyllis and I) eventually just lost touch because they did not have a phone for a long period of time.

Before I met Larry, I was already getting high and drinking. I started smoking marijuana and drinking when I was in high school. I eventually started smoking cocaine or crack as they called it. I was in my senior year of high school when I first experienced crack cocaine. I would smoke it with my friend Julia and sometimes Jodie. On some occasions Jodie and I would hook up with Julia and her boyfriend and smoke with them.

As time went on, my smoke friends increased. I was smoking crack cocaine when I met Larry. Larry was so demanding and aggressive and he would sometimes interrupt me when I was getting high with my get high buddies. I never did it around him or even discussed it with him but I know he had an idea. One day I had just finished getting high with my get high buddies and Larry came over. He just stared at me. I told him that I am going to be okay. Although I was doing drugs and was not living life as I should've and longed to, I always knew that I would recover and be alright.

I would get high for periods of time and just stop for periods of time. My get high buddies were in awe of that and the fact that I was able to do that. When I felt that I had gone too far with it, I would take a step back and get myself together. There were many times when I was not so proud of myself and two times in particular, I had went off the deep end, for me anyway. What I mean by that is I spent all of my money plus some. One thing I know is that after I was all done getting high and had no money, I felt terrible. I would work hard to do better and not spend all of my money but it was hard. The fact of the matter is that drugs just made you want more and more, to keep going and going.

I had eventually come up with a new way of handling myself when getting high. My motto was, don't let the drug control you, you control it. I did better but it was still hard. It took too much energy, trying to be in control of a drug. As time went on I became more and more distant from it until eventually I didn't use anymore. I realized that God was with me through all of it and he helped me to overcome that beast.

Larry's mom and dad were very friendly people. I loved to go over to their house. They didn't have anything so exciting but it was really calm, quiet and peaceful there, when I was there anyway. Larry's dad, Larry Sr. was extra kind to me. I began to see him as a father figure. Larry's mom, Rasheeda was a nice, soft spoken woman. Larry had an older brother, Jeff and the oldest of his siblings was his sister Kalilah.

All of his family were really nice to me. On occasions we would go to his grandmother's home on his father's side. They called her Madea. Madea reminded me of my Granny Brooks a little. Madea was a church going Christian woman who had birthed twelve children and had many grandchildren. Some of her children and grandchildren lived in her house.

Larry Sr. and I had grown very fond of one another. In fact, I would notice small things that made me believe that he was flirting and coming on to me. For instance, one day they were having a block club party and they invited us. We were all outside. I asked if I could go in and use their rest room. He proceeded to take me in as if I couldn't go on my own. His wife also came along. As we walked to the side door to enter the house, he asked me some friendly conversational questions. When we got to the door he opened it and just stood there staring in my eyes. It was really weird, especially since his wife stood there watching.

Another time we were at Kalilah's husband's parent's house for her daughter's birthday party. Larry Sr. propositioned me to dance with him and I did. During the dancing he hugged me and kissed me on my neck. I was really confused by this, again particularly with his wife being right there watching. I tried to convince myself that he was just being friendly although I knew in my heart that it was inappropriate and more than a friendly gesture. The toughest thing about the whole thing is that I kind of liked it and I wasn't sure how to place my feeling.

CHAPTER 12

After dating Larry for a couple of years I became pregnant with my second child. Prior to finding out I was pregnant with him I had been hired for a good job as an ORPD technician at Rush Presbyterian Hospital. The job involved cleaning and sterilizing the surgical instruments that were used by doctors during surgeries. The position was at a very prestigious hospital. I was given the information to report to orientation and instructions for going to take a drug test. A few days after I went to take the drug test and a few days before the orientation, a man called me from the place where the drug test was administered and told me that cocaine was found in my system. That was a total bummer.

I had not said no to drugs days before my drug test and that caused me a good job. The thing is that after that I really did not want to get high very much and I didn't. I felt that I needed to work on getting my life back on track. I soon realized that I was pregnant and went to see my doctor to get it confirmed and sure enough, I was pregnant.

My initial reaction was to get an abortion. I called around to find out how much abortion clinics were charging to perform a abortion. The strange thing was that everyone was quoting me prices far more than one thousand dollars. I knew that abortions were running about four hundred dollars or so at one time and I couldn't imagine that they were that much at that time. I would have to come up with this money to get the abortion and coming up with one thousand dollars or more seemed impossible at the time. I finally realized that it was not meant for me to get an abortion but it was meant for me to have my baby.

I knew that I needed to work and I applied for a job at Sesame Home Care as a personal care attendant (PCA). I was hired and while attending the orientation, I decided to go into the office during our lunch break and apply for a job as a supervisor. When I returned the application, the receptionist asked me to hold on a second, she went to the back and the manager came out with my application to interview me. She took me to her office and interviewed me and decided to hire me. I let her know that I was pregnant and she asked me to bring in a doctor statement indicating that it was okay for me to work. I did not finish the orientation and I started the job as a supervisor that Monday.

I liked my job at Sesame Home Care for the most part, although there were some issues in the office as it is in most workplaces. One thing that I really didn't like was how payroll were always messing up the PCA's checks. That was not cool at all. I stopped working and took my maternity leave when I turned nine months or thirty eight weeks. I wanted to prepare myself for giving birth to my son and I knew he would be coming any day.

There had been an accident with my uncle where he was rushed to the hospital. He was eventually taken to a hospital that specializes in neurology. My Granny Brooks had attempted to wake up my uncle after noticing that he was foaming at the nose and mouth. He would not wake up and so she called 911 for an ambulance. I had spent a night at Larry's house and had called Granny Brooks house and found out what had happened.

After going home and getting cleaned up, Larry took me to the hospital where my uncle and family were at. I decided to stay there with my family and told Larry he could leave. Later that night my uncle passed away. The next day my family and other people were at my grandmother's apartment which was downstairs from my apartment. That evening I began having contractions. The contractions eventually went away. My aunt Stacia was with me helping me to breathe. Larry was there too but was no help, only irritation and he eventually left. After the contractions calmed down, my aunt went home.

The very next evening, the contractions started again and this time it was the real thing. The contractions did not stop but started coming more frequently. I went to the hospital. My mom came to the hospital too. Larry and his dad were also there. Approximately twelve hours after I checked in the hospital, Rasheed Keleel Sampson was born at six pounds seven ounces.

Giving birth to Rasheed was a very different experience for me. Not only was I in labor for about 10 hours but I also had him full term and family was there to support me, all of which I did not experience when I gave birth to Christina. Although Jodie was at the hospital when I had Christina, he was not in the delivery room with me. I also got to see my baby while I was in the hospital and I took him home with me. When I had Christina she was immediately rushed to a hospital that was equipped to accommodate her needs due to premature birth.

I started off nursing Rasheed. I began to notice that he was having crying spells time after time after feeding him. Granny Brooks said that he had colic. I was not exactly sure what colic was but I soon found out that it was gas. I began to ask if I was supposed to burp him after feeding him. The few people that I asked said yes. I then realized that Rasheed had colic or gas because I had not been burping him after feeding him. For some strange reason, I did not think you had to burp babies that were breast fed.

CHAPTER 13

Rasheed was a good baby. Christina took to him well. While I was pregnant with Rasheed I had an interview at a Day Care Center called Little People Palace. Christina went to Little People Palace when she was preschool age. They were in a new location now about six streets away from where they previously were. The director/co owner Judith Long asked me when my due date was and I told her.

I was excited to get a call from her about four weeks after I had Rasheed. I took the job and had to tell my manager at Sesame Home Care that I would not be coming back. They were angry. It was really weird, especially considering a person had a right to change their mind or change jobs. Little People Palace was closer to home and the baby sitter that I took Rasheed to, and I thought that would work out fine.

I enjoyed working at Little People Palace in spite of a few unpleasant elements there. I actually stayed there for a whole year. I started there in September of 1997 and left in August of 1998. At the end of the regular school year in June, there was a graduation ceremony for all of the children. The kindergarten children were graduating and going on to first grade at new schools. The graduation ceremony took place on a Saturday. After the ceremony was over, my coworkers were asking one another about their checks. We would normally get our checks on Friday but Mrs. Long said that we would get them Saturday after the graduation ceremony.

After noticing that the employees were concerned and ready to get there checks, I suggested that someone ask Mrs. Long about their check. No one would go to Mrs. Long. Once I got done doing the cleaning I was doing, I was ready to get my check and leave. I went and asked Mrs. Long if I could have my check and she said "common sense should tell you that you all won't get your checks until we have cleaned up". When she said that all I heard in my head was common sense is telling me that it's time for me to leave this job.

The thing was that Mrs. Long did not tell us that we had to clean up and then we would get our checks. Expectations for us to clean up were never mentioned, not that it was an issue. The fact of the matter is that we helped anyway and we were done so I really didn't get where she was coming from. On top of all of that, she said "common sense...". I did not think that was appropriate at all and I no longer wanted to work there, which is why I began to look for a new job.

I did get a new job and was expected to start the week after the last day of the summer session. I told Mrs. Long that I would be attending an orientation that following Monday and that I would not be there. That orientation turned into me starting a new job the following day. I started the job that Tuesday and had not called to tell Mrs. Long that I would not be back. I tried to reason in my mind that I told her that I was going to an orientation so she should have known that it was to start a new job. I was doing what she did. Common sense should have told her if I was going to an orientation, I was starting a new job.

The truth is that I didn't have the guts to tell her that I would not be back. I ended up calling her at the end of the week. I apologized for not calling her sooner to let her know that I would not be back. I felt that I should be responsible and clearly tell her that I had a new job. Mrs. Long responded by saying that the children were going to be disappointed. The thing is that people have a right to move on, change jobs, leave jobs, etc. I felt that Mrs. Long was trying to make me feel guilty about leaving. Later, in life I learned that that was a form of manipulation, emotional manipulation that is, trying to make me feel guilty. On a subconscious level I believe that is why I initially avoided telling her.

The new job was at a recycling plant. Garbage trucks throughout the city would bring their garbage trucks to the recycling plant to dump the garbage on the conveyor belt. My job was to remove plastic, cardboard, paper, etc., depending on where I was stationed. It smelled really bad in that place and I really tried to stick it out. I also realized that as an employee there you were pretty much forced to work overtime.

We started at 6:00am and depending on how much more garbage was coming in determined when we got off. I did not like the idea of being made to work twelve hour shifts. I did it for the first week and it was not that great particularly because I needed to get my son from day care by 6:00pm. I worked around it the first week but was not happy about how this was going. Although I was not happy with the new job, I did not regret leaving Little People Palace Day Care. I knew it was time for me to move on from there.

The following week I went to work at the recycling plant. On Tuesday, the second workday of the week, I felt really sick and was tired of smelling that garbage. I could not take it anymore. That job just was not for me. I left my position and went to the manager's office and told him I could no longer work there. He asked if I just wanted to take the day or week off and come back and try it again. I told him no. He had me fill out a form indicating that I could come back if I wanted to because I left in good standing. I knew when I left there that I would never be back. It was just too much! At least I tried, I thought.

Soon after I started working at the United States Postal Services (USPS). One day it was really tough out there delivering mail because of all the snow. When I came into the station I was talking smack and said I quit. I verbalized it loud so that everyone could hear me. It was pay day that day and I was getting my first check. My manager handed me my check, I opened the envelope and when I saw the amount of my check, I told him that I would be back tomorrow. I went from quitting to coming back tomorrow. I guess you can say that my check was very encouraging. It was like a tax refund check for me.

I had never made that much money from working a job. Although I knew how much the pay rate was, I never calculated it to be that much. I never really thought about it at all. I was just happy to be working and getting a check. After looking at my check stub I realized that a lot of the pay came from time and a half for every hour worked after forty hours per week. I never thought about the overtime but looking at it on my check was really cool!

CHAPTER 14

One day I was watching television and there had been announcements concerning registering for testing for the United States Post Office (USPS) in the state of Illinois. I decided to write down the telephone number and call. I called and answered all of the questions. A couple of weeks later I received a letter indicating when and where to go for testing. I went to take the test and ended up getting another letter in the mail stating that I had passed the test and was up for consideration to be hired. Soon after, I received a letter to come their facilities to have a physical and take a drug test.

I was so happy and proud to take that drug test because I had not gotten high in quite a while. It felt good to be taking a drug test knowing that I was clean and not having to consider an alternative to passing it. Sure enough, I passed the physical and drug test and was later given instructions on where to report for the one week training. That's how I ended up working at the post office.

Training lasted for one week and the following week I started working at one of the stations on the West Side of Chicago. It was quite a way from where I lived but I did it. I saw it as a great opportunity. Things were going pretty good. I was being moved around to different routes at first and then I was becoming regular on certain routes that had no assigned mail carrier. I actually liked the routes and had become very familiar with them.

I was getting pretty good at the job and had not had any complaints. All of a sudden the job seemed to be too much for me and I would just break down sometimes and cry. It was winter and the snow and the cold made it really difficult. One day I was working a different route than my usual routes and I wanted to just quit. I called Larry and he talked me into staying. He asked me where I was and I told him. He came to find me and helped me deliver the mail. Larry was working at a post office delivering mail when I met him, so he knew the ropes.

After a while the head manager of the station pulled up on us. I explained to him that I wanted to quit and called my boyfriend and he came to help me. I told him that he had worked for USPS before, delivering mail. My manager was cool but he told me that my boyfriend needed to leave. I figured that someone must have called the station and reported something pertaining to us. I never was sure what it was.

I was motivated for a while but after some time I felt unfulfilled. I had to drive and sit in traffic on my way to work and coming home from work. It was the winter season and had been snowing. City trucks would drive through the city in salt trucks distributing salt on the streets. The salt had caused a lot of potholes in the streets and these potholes were on the expressway as well. This made traffic absolutely unbearable, for me anyway and only added to the unpleasant feelings I was already having. Looking back at that time I realize that I just had a lot of emotional, unresolved issues. No matter what I did, where I worked or what I made, I would always have this underlying feeling of unhappiness.

One day on my way home from work, I was thinking about New Port cigarettes. I had not smoked in quite a while. The next thing I knew, I was at the gas station buying Newport cigarettes in the box. Soon after that I found myself wanting to get high again. It was about a few days or so after I bought those cigarettes that I contacted one of the girls that I used to get high with. That evening I met her at a friend of hers house and got high with them. I did not stop there.

I was back getting high and as I already stated it was really due to that underlying feeling of unhappiness. That's why they say that when you have internal pain, particularly from childhood dramas and experiences, people tend to try to escape the pain by taking drugs, alcohol or being promiscuous. I had experienced escaping pain by indulging in all three of these activities.

CHAPTER 15

One day after dropping my children off at the day care provider, I was on the expressway on my way to work. The traffic was worse than the normal bad traffic. After a snow fall, city workers had once again distributed salt to clear the ice on the roads and the after effects were more potholes. These potholes were everywhere on the expressway and so it made the traffic much worse.

I was not happy about going through this to get to the other side of town to work. On my way to work one day I started crying really bad and eventually decided that I was not going back to that job. The other unpleasant thing was that because of the snow fall and the snow on the ground, it was much harder to deliver the mail. It took a lot longer and I had been experiencing frost bite on my feet and hands.

The manager tended to give the heavier loads to the new people. The new people at the station where I worked were all considered subs, which meant that we were not regular employees. Our contract was for a year and after that year we would find out if they wanted to keep us as regular employees. The attitude that the two women supervisors tried to implant in our minds was that as a newbie, we just had to get dogged. I could not take on that mentality.

Taking all of this into consideration, I got off of the express way at the next exit and went home. When I got home, I called the station to tell the supervisor on site that I would not be back. She told me that was a good job. I told her that it is not a good job, its good money. She said, "you're right". She continued to call me for some time after that along with the male manager of the station, asking me to come back and I declined every time. Eventually, she told me to come and get my check on pay day and to bring my employee ID. I did that and when I got there she had me sign a document indicating that I left on good terms and that I could come back. This seemed to be becoming a pattern.

I was relieved that I was not working at the Post Office anymore. I had less stress. The only problem was that I was getting high. I ended up getting back on welfare and that was how I survived for a while. After several months I had decided that I had enough of that mess and knew it was time for me to get my life back on track. I stopped getting high so much and started looking for a job.

Larry was helping to take care of things financially so it was not too big of a deal. After Rasheed was born, Larry stayed at my apartment more and more. His things accumulated in my apartment too. After a while it was clear that he had moved in. There was never any discussion about it. I saw what was happening and I said nothing. I guess I was okay with it. After all, we really had become a family.

CHAPTER 16

My teenager cousin, Ciera was living in my apartment too. Ciera was in foster care, along with her sisters and brothers. They were all split up. Ciera was the oldest and she was on her way to a group home for foster children. I had heard some unpleasant stories about those places and did not want to see her end up there, so I decided I would take her in. I became her foster parent. This all happened about a month or so before Rasheed was born.

I only cared for her for almost a year because she started getting out of control. She was already somewhat of a troubled child, and I dealt with her as best as I could but when she started staying out over night, I knew that was the end of her being in my care. One night she did not come home and I did not search for her. The following morning, I called the foster care agency we were assigned to and explained to her case worker that she did not come home and that I am not looking for her anymore. I told him that when they find her they can keep her. I made it clear that she was no longer welcome in my home.

The interesting thing is that I had put Larry out about a month prior to this. Things had gotten out of control with him too. The thing was that he wanted to control me and he really needed to control himself. I no longer wanted to argue, fight, or deal with the situation. It was draining and I needed some peace. One night when Larry was in a rage, I called the police and told them that he was no longer welcome in my home. You would think that was the end but as I said before, not with Larry. He was not easy to get rid of!

Eventually, I applied for a job at Flemmings Community Center. A friend of mine told me that they were hiring for a preschool assistant teacher. Her son was enrolled in one of their preschool programs. The day I went there to apply, I was also given a test, a questionnaire, and I had an interview. When I left there, I headed home. A few minutes after I arrived home, I received a call from the woman that interviewed me, offering me the job.

That worked out well for the most part. I was making decent money and sure enough after a while I started getting high more. After some issues at the Day Care where Rasheed was going at the time, I enrolled him at Flemmings Day Care at the site where I worked. Initially, he was in the class that I was in but I realized that he needed to be somewhere else so it was agreed that he could move to another class.

Prior to getting the job at Flemmings Day Care, I had an on and off relationship with Larry, mostly on in his mind. During one of our off times he had started dating a young lady named Marcia. Marcia worked with him and Larry told me that she would make comments to him after he would get off the telephone angry with me. I guess she convinced him that he should be with her so he wouldn't have to be arguing all the time.

The truth is that we were not always necessarily arguing. Most of the time Larry did not like what I was saying or did not like that I would not do and behave the way he wanted me to so that angered him. I guess Marcia was willing to do and be what Larry wanted her to do and be. During one of our off periods he began to date her. Who knows, he may not have even waited to our off period and it really didn't matter because it was about time for things to change and if Marcia was there to assist in the transition that was just fine with me.

Larry and I were broke up for about seven months. During that time I dated other people. I also had sexual relations with Larry sometimes. There came a time when I became pregnant. There was one guy named Julius that I was seeing quite often. When I came up pregnant, I really believed that the baby was his but I knew that it was a possibility that it could have been Larry's.

Julius and I became distant and were not seeing or talking very much. I did tell him that I was pregnant and after that it seemed like that was the deal breaker. When I was about five months pregnant, my water broke and I went to the hospital. I had lost the baby. I was really relieved because I really did not want to have the baby but I wanted to be responsible and do what I needed to do since I had got myself into that situation.

I called one of Julius's friends in an attempt to contact Julius a few weeks after I lost the baby. He called me about a week later, He wanted to talk about the baby and I told him that I was not pregnant anymore. I did not see Julius again until about five months after that and that was pretty much the last time I saw him.

When he came by, I did not like what I saw. He was a little more needy than he was when I last saw him. He did not want to leave my apartment. I had to make him leave and I never saw him again, although he called me. I pretty much had to let him know that he needed to move on. Julius was looking for someone to take care of him and I was not that girl.

A few months after that Larry came to me and told me that he knew he had not done all the right things when we were together and that he realized that. He said that he was a different person and asked me for another chance. I thought about it and eventually decided I would try it again. He was still with Marcia when he asked for another chance. Later, he told me that when he told Marcia that he wanted to get back with me and try and work it out, she started crying and told him that she was pregnant.

I really felt bad for her and was not sure if it was a good idea for us to get back together. I figured she needed him now but Larry was persistent about rekindling and restoring our relationship, so I went along with it. As far as I know, Larry and Marcia did not have contact throughout her pregnancy. I ended up getting pregnant myself and when I tell you that baby made me sick, I thought it was literally killing me. I decided to have an abortion. For one, I could not continue with how sick I was and I really did not want another child with Larry. Although I had agreed to rekindle our relationship, I was still skeptical of his mental stability.

CHAPTER 17

One day I called Larry's cell phone and he had a greeting for his voice mail with a rap on it saying "you got played and I think you know it". It spoke of a person trying to play them but they got played instead. Larry and I had recently had a slight altercation and so I thought he put that on his greeting for me. When I asked him about it he said he had that on there for Marcia. I immediately took offense to it. It made me terribly angry to know that she was carrying his child and he was busy playing games about who's playing who. I thought it was very immature and uncaused for. After all, there was an unborn baby involved. A life that is, and that is not a thing to be played with.

I went off on Larry and I was very disgusted with him and I told him so. A short time after that Larry told me that Marcia's relatives called him and told him that Marcia had the baby and that it was a boy. I really don't know what Larry was on or what he was really doing but he wanted me to believe that he had not seen the baby. Although I did not verbalize my thoughts or feelings, I did not think it was cool if that was really the case.

I had decided to go back to school. I took two classes in the evening while I continued to work during the day. I had already completed quite a bit of course work for my degree before taking a break. I wanted to finish but I did not want to overwhelm myself, so I took it easy. The first semester I was back in school, Larry agreed to come and watch Christina and Rasheed for a few hours while I went to class. It was only two nights a week.

I would call home during my break to check on them and most of the time Larry would not even be there. The thing is that he would be there when I got home. It seemed that he would get there just in time to see me. I was not okay with that because the point was for him to be there to supervise them. Although Christina was old enough to watch Rasheed a little bit, she still needed an adult to watch her. I figured if Larry would be on his way, I could leave them at home alone for a little bit until Larry arrived.

I asked Larry about it and he told me he could not do it because it was getting in the way of his music. My Uncle Kody lived downstairs from me with Granny Brooks. He was free at the time. He was not working. I asked him if he could just make sure they were okay and I could pay him for checking on them from time to time. He agreed.

Soon after that, Larry and I got into a huge fight and I was pretty much done with him. We hadn't spoken for over a week and when I finally heard from him he told me that Marcia and the baby were living with him in his apartment. I realized that after I had not tried to reach out to him or respond to his attempts of reaching out to me, he decided to contact Marcia and move her and the baby in to get back at me. The truth is that I never looked back again. Although it hurt a little, I was ready to move on from him and so I did nothing. I did not want any more of the drama that came with Larry. I wish it were that simple.

A couple of weeks later, my uncle Mitch had been admitted into the hospital. Mitch's blood pressure had dropped really low and soon after he had passed away. A year or so prior to Mitch's passing, I could sense his death coming. Furthermore, I could sense his desire to die. I knew that Mitch was ready to go. He had custody of his two children who had special needs and had raised two older children too before they moved out on their own.

Uncle Mitch had a drug problem. His drug of choice was heroin and he may have tampered with cocaine and crack as well. He would drink but he was more about the drugs. When I was a little girl he used to drink MD 20/20 which is a cheap wine. He would tell my cousin (his daughter) and I that it was his medicine, and like believing children we believed him until we got old enough to understand what his medicine really was.

The day of Uncle Mitch's funeral and burial, my aunts took Granny Brooks to the emergency room. Granny Brooks had a heart attack. My aunts noticed that she didn't seem right and had decided to take her to the hospital. It may have been a bit much for her having just buried her son after burying another one just a couple years earlier. It's hard to lose anyone you love and I can only imagine that burying your child can be devastating. Granny Brooks was a very strong woman and even she had her breaking point.

Granny Brook came home from the hospital, having a date to return for heart surgery. Granny Brooks arteries were clogged and that was not good for her heart. That made it difficult for blood to be pumped to her heart. Granny Brooks stayed at Aunt Stacia's house so that she could keep a close eye on her. I was all out of balance and did my very best to cope with the situation. Granny Brooks ended up having to be taken back to the hospital before her scheduled surgery date because she was having pain in her chest.

The day before her surgery, my mom called me while she was at the hospital visiting. She told me that Granny Brooks wanted to talk to me. I just broke down crying. See, I had not been to see Granny Brooks. I did not like the idea of her having surgery. I was really afraid that if she had surgery, she was going to die. I told my mother that Granny could just take some herbs that could clear her arteries and she did not have to have the surgery. I had become very familiar with and fond of herbal and natural remedies since I had been dealing with Larry and his family. His parents were very much into herbs and were distributors for Nature Sunshine Products.

When Granny Brooks got on the phone, the first thing she said to me was aren't you going to miss me? Again, I broke down crying. That was her way of letting me know that she would be making her transition soon. Although I didn't like it, I had no other choice but to work through it.

CHAPTER 18

After Granny Brooks surgery, I went to see her and I broke down again. I broke down crying. She was swollen and had tubes everywhere. I had never seen my Granny this way. I rarely went to see her while she was in the hospital. I went about two more times after that. Granny Brooks never fully recovered from that operation. After a while, she was admitted into a nursing home.

The nursing home that Granny Brooks was in was quite a ways from the city where we lived. My mom went to see her regularly, if not every day, every other day for sure. Sometimes I went with her. Granny had been in the nursing home for a few months and her condition had not improved. She was bedridden and everything had to be done for her. I started noticing that Granny Brook's eyes were turning green blue and they were glassy. I knew that it was just a matter of time before Granny Brooks would make her transition.

One night I was sleeping and I had a premonition that Granny Brooks had made her transition. Early that morning my telephone rang and I went to answer it although I was half sleep. It was my Aunt Linda. She said that Aunt Stacia had received a call from the nursing home but she wasn't sure what was going on. She indicated that they needed to go to the nursing home to find out what was going on. She asked me if she could drop off Stacia's children along with her son. I told her to bring them. I already knew that Granny

Brooks had made her transition. Later, Aunt Linda called to inform me that Granny Brooks had passed away.

Relatives from all over the country came in town for Granny Brook's funeral. Some of my male cousins hung out with me in my apartment. I was taking summer classes at Chicago State University at the time. The day before the funeral, I received a stipend check in the mail from Chicago State University. I went and cashed my check and went to the liquor store and bought a gallon of Hennessy. I had never had Hennessey before. My cousin Markus talked about it a lot. It seemed to be his choice of drink. Although it was way more expensive than I would normally pay for liquor, I bought it. It was a special time. We were saying good bye to Granny Brooks. That night my cousins and I partied in my apartment. The morning of the funeral, I woke up with a hangover. I was very disappointed in myself. I could not be out of it for my Granny's funeral.

Everything went well and I made it through with no signs of having a hangover. That's what I thought anyway. The funeral and repass was at Saga Temple Church and we had another repass later at Granny Brooks apartment. Everything went well and all of the family that came from out of state returned home over the next few days.

CHAPTER 19

At the end of the summer session of classes, I knew I had not performed well. I was taking History 101 and Philosophy 101. I had already failed the midterm test in History and had not felt much better about taking the final. I did okay in philosophy but at the end of the semester we had a debate and a paper due. For the debate there were two sides, pro abortion and anti abortion. It really didn't matter which side I was on because I felt like I could argue both sides. I did not jump on either side at first but when it came down to having to pick a side, the pro abortion side was short so I decided to join them.

I felt like I did really well in the debate and I had used some of the fallacies that we learned in the earlier part of the class. When I did this the lecture hall became tense and everyone acted as if I were saying something wrong. The students were kind of smiling and the instructor looked angry. I learned that the instructor felt like I was challenging him. The twisted thing was the instructor was angry because I was able to apply the fallacies in my argument.

Shouldn't I have been allowed to apply those principles? The truth is that although the instructor seemed to be intimidated by my ability to do that, I later learned that I was being egotistical and I was flaunting my abilities. That was not cool on my part. My argument for abortion was really good too! I guess it was just too much and the instructor felt that a student of his should not be able to understand and articulate this knowledge above him, only what he had given and that should have been it. Years later, I started to see this same behavior in many people in my life.

I did not do my paper for my Philosophy class. I was too busy distracting myself with other things and had a hard time focusing on school work or writing that paper. I believe that I had not properly grieved Granny Brooks death and I was stuck somewhere in that process, that had not properly taken place. I ended up getting an F in History and a D in Philosophy.

I had been on academic probation and had to see a counselor for the Fall Semester. Getting those F's raised the University's eyebrows and they sensed trouble. Their policy for my situation entailed that I see a counselor on campus once a week. I started seeing a counselor and that helped me a lot. In counseling, I realized that I had not allowed myself to grieve Granny Brook's death. Although I knew she was gone, it was surreal.

I knew Granny was going to make her transition before she did but I still hadn't gotten a grip on the fact that she was no longer on the physical plane. I believe it was because life was different without Granny Brooks and I never knew life without her before then. Granny was there when I was born and had always been there. She had been such a vital part of my life. She was a major life force and source for me. I felt somewhat out of place once she was gone but at the same time I felt strong and sturdy. I had to readjust and continue the path that Granny Brooks helped to ground me in.

God used Granny Brooks in my life in such a tremendous way. God had her in my life to embed some sound Godly principles in me. The fact that I even knew of God was because of Granny Brooks. The rest of my life would be about building those principles that had been planted within me.

CHAPTER 20

I moved to my mother's house during the summer. My cousin was selling the building and even though she had not sold it yet, I was ready to leave. It was a bit much for me to stay there after the passing of Granny Brooks. It was time for me to move on and my mother said that I could come to her house and so I did. I continued attending classes at Chicago State University in the fall. I eventually started working at Gracious Home Care. I worked as a Home Health Aide. I really liked my job and my clients were cool.

One day I went to my friends Angel house. I had not spoken to Angel in a while. I was staying at her house for a short while over the summer and things didn't go so well. This happened the following summer after moving in with my mom and her husband. Angel and I were getting high together again and as usual one day I decided that I could not continue to live that way. I left and I did not talk to her for a while until I wanted to get high again.

I called Angel and went over to her mom's house and was told that she was across the street at Marvin's house. Marvin was a guy that used to live in the basement of the building where Angel stayed at with her mother and sister. Marvin would let us get high at his old house, and he moved across the street and let us get high at his new house too. Marvin got high too. Angel and I were cool as if we had never separated. It was no problem, especially considering the fact that we were about to get high.

After we had smoked so much, I had no more money with me so I decided to catch a cab to my mom's house to get some more. I called a cab and while I was waiting on the cab, I looked out the window and noticed a cab parking. I asked the driver was he here for me. He said no but asked me if I needed a ride. I said yes and he said come on. I went down stairs and got in the cab. He took me to my mom's house. His name was Aaron.

When Aaron dropped me back off at Marvin's house he gave me his telephone number and asked me if I could come and hang out with him later. I said yes and when I was done getting high and I thought I had given myself enough time to calm down and seem normal, I called Aaron and walked around the corner to his apartment. Aaron did not waste much time letting me know that he was interested in sex. That was no issue for me. I figured that sex had something to do with us hooking up. We had sex that night and continued to have sex regularly. Angel and I continued to get high regularly too. Every now and then we would be with another one of our get high partners but for the most part Angel and I were tight just like it was before.

I really liked Aaron, or so I thought I did. There was something about his swag that really turned me on. He was African and I was kind of crushing on Africans around that time. Our relationship was just sex to Aaron. Although I think he kind of liked me, it was not enough to really commit to me. One day he said that he had too much going on at the time to be in a committed relationship. He was a full time student, he worked full time, and he played soccer regularly. He certainly had a lot going on and was not interested in committing, not to me anyway.

Eventually, I realized that I was pregnant. I went to the clinic and after taking a pregnancy test I was told that I was pregnant. Prior to hearing that I was pregnant, I did not feel sick, although I felt pregnant. Later that evening I told Aaron that I was pregnant. He said that he used condoms and I said I know and things happen. He asked me if I was sure that it was his baby and I said yes. He told me to get an abortion. I told him no and I hung up.

I went on about my business without being in communication with him. I was hurt to the core but I was determined to be strong, have my baby and take care of it and that's just what I did. I had been working at Gracious Home Care and attending classes at Chicago State University. I had been feeling pain while working and decided I needed to stop working until after I had my baby. I resigned from Gracious Home Care and continued to go to school.

A week after I stopped working, I had some complications. My water bag broke and I was devastated. Although I had no support from Aaron, I loved my baby and I wanted it! I pouted and cried after my water bag broke and my mother comforted me. She said we are going to think positive and believe in the life of my baby. I agreed with her and we headed to the hospital. I really appreciate my mom for helping me through that tough place.

Late that night I was transferred to a hospital that was equipped to handle premature births and babies. Cook County Hospital was well known for great care with premature babies. Initially the doctors had decided to try to hold the baby in me for as long as possible. I was only 24 weeks along. I was really concerned about getting back to school but I wanted my baby to be okay too. I ended up with a fever and my labor had to be induced.

After being at Cook County Hospital for about two days, I gave birth to a baby girl. Freedom Keann Brooks. Freedom was 1 pound 10 ounces. She was very small. She was smaller than Christina was when she was born. Freedom stayed in the hospital for three months and three days before I was able to bring her home. When I finally brought her home from the hospital, she was five pounds.

CHAPTER 21

While Freedom was in the hospital, I went to see her quite a bit. I would attend classes and work around my classes and school work to go and visit her. When I didn't go to see her, I would call and check on her. Christina and Rasheed were excited about their baby sister. Christina had gone with me a couple of times to see her. She even held her once. Rasheed was too young to go to the intensive care prenatal unit where she was.

When Freedom came home I continued to take my classes. In fact, I had taken a class that summer and was at the end of that class when she came home. Christina helped out a lot with Freedom. Freedom was the baby sister that Christina always wanted. I stayed at my mom's house for quite some time after having Freedom. I shared a room with my three children.

When I came to move in my mom's house, we brought Christina's bunk bed. The bottom bed was full size and the top bunk was twin size. Christina slept on the top bunk and Rasheed would sleep on the bottom bunk with me when he was there. Rasheed went back and forth between Larry and I. He had him for a week and I had him for a week. We pretty much shared custody. When Freedom came home, she slept in the crib part of her playpen/crib.

Although I was no longer with Larry, we continued to be friends. Many times I felt that I would be his friend to keep the peace. The thing is that every time there was something happening with

Larry that I was not okay with, he would want to go to war with me because I would pull back and distance myself from him. He absolutely did not like it when I did not want to engage with him anymore. I guess he felt rejected but I always wondered how was it that he felt that I was supposed to just do whatever he wanted me to do. I just didn't get it.

One day my mom, Christina, Rasheed, Freedom and I were coming in from my cousins baby shower. As we were coming in the house Rasheed was half sleep and leaned against the wall right outside the front door. I had to pull him in because he was sleep. As we walked into the house, my stepfather Tony spoke to us. I spoke back and the next thing I know is that he pushed Rasheed out the door saying "he needs to speak to me". I put the car seat down with Freedom in it, went and got my son from outside and flipped out.

First of all he was sleep and that was so obvious. Secondly, Tony is a grown man and he pushed a six year old sleeping boy out the door because he didn't speak. He really had issues, particularly with his manhood and that definitely was not the way to resolve it. Later in life, I learned that his ego was over active. I called my Aunt Stacia and told her what happened and said I got to get out of here. I was very emotional and intense. She said that she would call me back and when she did she told me that my cousin Dina said that her Aunt said that I can come and stay in her apartment where my Uncle Harold was staying.

Aunt Stacia came and got me and took me to the apartment. The apartment was on the first floor in a two flat building. Dina's aunts name was Bernadine. Bernadine was staying on the second floor at the time. Her mom had always lived on the second floor and she had gotten sick a few years ago. Bernadine started staying upstairs in her mother's apartment to be closer to her, to take better care of her. Her mom had passed away about a year before I came and Bernadine was still staying up there, with intentions to eventually come back downstairs to her apartment.

After my cousin Maggie sold the family building, my Uncle Harold came to stay in a room in Bernadine's apartment. Uncle Harold pretty much had the downstairs apartment to himself because Bernadine had been staying upstairs. When I came, I stayed in Bernadine's room. Freedom and I slept in the room, while Christina and Rasheed slept on the couches in the front room. Bernadine told me that I could stay there until November because she would be coming back downstairs. Bernadine would go to the doctor a lot around the end of October and she passed away after being admitted into the hospital during one of her doctor visits. I was very sorry to hear that Bernadine had passed away.

CHAPTER 22

My cousin Dina was now the heir of that building. She was the last family member on her father's side of the family. Dina told me that I could stay there. She also said that she would be selling the building. She indicated that I could stay there until she sold it.

The building was really old and kind of raggedy and dusty. I did not care. I really appreciated having a place to stay for my children and myself. I made good with what we had. I cleaned up really good on a regular basis. I continued taking classes and I was living there when I completed my degree program and graduated. In spite of all of the obstacles and challenges, I kept the faith and continued to press on. The thing is that the circumstances just made me have to adjust some things and not quit all together and that's just what I did. I even put Freedom in a Day Care around the corner from where we were staying. I made it work and God worked it out.

During the time that we were staying on 90th Street, my aunt Pauline stayed with us for a while. Pauline had nine children, which were in foster care or on their own. She had one child with her. When her children were put in foster care, she was pregnant and so she only had that child in her care. Her name was Selby. Aunt Pauline was deep into drugs and drinking. She was not very stable and would live from place to place.

She came by the building a day before Thanksgiving to visit. She ended up spending the night and spending Thanksgiving with the whole family. She never left and was pretty much living there. Aunt Pauline would always ask for money and she would also ask me to watch Selby. I watched Selby most of the time. She would ask to borrow money and sometimes I would loan it to her.

One of Aunt Pauline's drugs of choice was crack cocaine. I had been a previous crack cocaine user. There was a lot of drama going on to the point where I wanted to leave the apartment. I explained this to Uncle Harold and he insisted that Aunt Pauline would have to leave. The thing is that Aunt Pauline didn't contribute any money to any bills or expenses and I did! Uncle Harold did not want to have all the bills on him alone. He knew Aunt Pauline would not help and really had no means of contributing. Uncle Harold eventually asked Aunt Pauline to leave and she left after a dramatic performance.

I had been going to church down the street from where we were staying. I was really passionate about nurturing my relationship with God. Before my Aunt Pauline left, I started feeling like I wanted to get high with crack cocaine. Before I knew it, I was getting high again. It was something about her being there and knowing that she was using that affected me. It was like the crack spirit had transferred to me and the kicker was that I was already familiar with it. Sometimes, I would go to church and come home and get high. It was kind of crazy ridiculous. The thing is that I was really sincere about loving and serving God. I know for sure that God was with me and he carried me through that crazy period in my life. I am so grateful that God knew my heart and loved me so much.

I graduated from Chicago State University in May. I graduated with a 2.9 GPA. It could have been a 3.0 if I had gotten a B in my drawing class. The instructor emphasized that we needed to be there on the last day of class for a project that could greatly affect our grade. I had money and I wanted to get high so bad that I ditched class and went to my friend Neecy's house to get high. Missing that class did cost me. I truly believe that if I had gone to the last day of class and completed the last project, I would have gotten a B in the class and my GPA would have been 3.0 instead of 2.9.

Soon after graduating from Chicago State University, I learned that my cousin Dina had sold the building and we needed to be leaving by the first of July. I had no idea what I was going to do. I ended up going to my friend Neecy's house to stay. I paid her rent for the month and gave her money to get a home telephone turned on so we could have a land line telephone. Of course, we got high but by the second day I had had enough. I was not comfortable with the living situation and getting high did not make it better.

Mice would come out of the kitchen and walk right up to our feet as if they were pets. When I saw this happening I asked Neecy did she see the mice. She said that she just ignore them. I was baffled and I could not ignore the mice. The building that I had just moved from had mice too. They didn't show themselves right away. It took a while. When they did, I got mouse poisin and moth balls to combat and kill them. That worked for a while but then the mice came out full fledged and they were adamant about letting it be known that we were in there house. I was ready to get out of there.

My pastor at the time allowed me to store most of my things in a storage area behind the church and once I got the okay to stay with Neecy, I was out of there only to run into the same problems. Not only were the mice an issue but all Neecy wanted to do was get high. I liked to get high but I liked to take a break too! Neecy's daughter's birthday was on the second day that I was there. We got high earlier and after a while, I thought that we needed to do something to celebrate her daughter's birthday.

Neecy said that she had ordered her a cake from the grocery store down the street. She could not seem to slow down long enough to get the things for her daughter's birthday celebration. I agreed to go to the grocery store to get her cake and other food to give her a birthday party. Neecy gave me her food stamp card and I went to the store with all the children to shop for the birthday party. The next day I realized that I could not continue to live there. It was not going to work. All Neecy wanted to do was get high. I was already in a situation that I needed to improve and getting high like that would only make matters worse. It got to the point that I did not want to get high any more.

CHAPTER 23

I called my pastor and told him that I could not stay where I was and I had no place to go. He came and got me and my children and took us to a hotel. That was on a Saturday. He came and got us Sunday morning and we went to church. After church, my pastor and his wife decided that we could stay at their house.

I really appreciated my pastor and his wife for letting me stay at their home. Things were cool and I was somewhat comfortable. They lived far away from the city and you either had to have a car to get to the city or it would take at least two hours traveling on public transportation. This meant that I had to depend on them to get around for the most part. It was not really a big deal at first. I was not trying to go into the city so much. I found myself hanging around the house most of the time. I kind of needed a breather and so I took it.

I was receiving food stamps and I bought food for the house. They did not really have food and it appeared that they did not buy food regularly. I was not used to that and my children and I were used to eating regularly. The cool thing was that I only had Christina and Freedom with me now. After an incident at Neecy's house with her son and Rasheed, I asked Larry to keep him. Larry was adamant about letting me know that he most definitely would keep him. The incident happened the first day we were there and so the second day,

I met Larry to take Rasheed to him. By the third day when I decided I could no longer stay there, Rasheed was in Larry's care.

That all worked out great. Now here we were in another challenging situation. The house was rather chaotic and unstructured. My pastor and his wife had several foster children. Two were their relatives and two were not. The oldest girl was thirteen and she was my pastor's granddaughter. She mostly took care of the other children who were nine, three, and two years old. It was a lot for a thirteen year old girl. I could relate to her situation because it reminded me of how I took care of my two little brothers. In fact, I had my youngest brother so much that people thought he was my son.

I bought food for the house and spent quite a bit of money. I bought enough for the whole house. I couldn't just buy food for my children and I. The food went so fast that I knew I could not keep doing that. After being there a couple of weeks, I decided I needed to find somewhere else to go. I called the mother of one of Christina's friends named Tina, who I was cool with and asked her if I could stay at her house for a little while. She said that we could come.

Rasheed's birthday was coming and Larry and I decided to take him out for his birthday. We met at a place called the Kids Spot to celebrate Rasheed's birthday. I had brought quite a bit of our things with us when we came to the city because I planned to transition to Tina's after we celebrated Rasheed's birthday. That evening when I tried to call Tina she would not answer. I kept calling and finally someone answered and said she was not there. I realized that she had decided that she did not want us to come to her house but did not want to verbally tell me. I got the picture.

I ended up asking Aunt Stacia if I could store my things at her house so that I could go to a shelter and get my things later once I got situated. That is what I did but the thing is that when my children and I went to the station where you go when you are homeless and are looking to get into a shelter, after sitting there for a while, they said that they had no openings. The clinic where we were would be closing in a while and we would have to leave there so we left and went back to my mom's house. I did not know what we were going to do. It occurred to me to ask my Aunt Stacia if we could come to her house.

I called Aunt Stacia when we got to my mother's and told her the situation and asked her if we could come to her house. She told me that she needed to speak to her husband and get back to me. When she got back to me she told me that her husband said that my stepfather and I needed to repair our relationship. As weird as I thought that the statement was, I took it as direction to keep moving forward.

That Sunday I had been talking on the telephone while I was on the porch at my mom's house. I had been discussing the situation and trying to determine what I could do now. When I came inside, Tony told me that this was my home and I take care of it and no one had told me to leave anyway. Obviously, he heard my side of the conversation when I was talking on the telephone.

Although I thought it was crazy that what had transpired when I left was good reason to leave, he thought it was no need for me to leave. Furthermore, I thought that I had a choice as to whether or not I need to leave somewhere. I didn't realize that I had to have permission to lead my own life. As crazy as that whole statement was, I had to humble myself and be cool because I was homeless and he was telling me I could stay at home, as he put it. I told him thank you and I stayed. I was very relieved.

CHAPTER 24

I began looking for a job and had interviewed with the owner of a Day Care Center. The lady, Ms. Tape was opening three new Day Care Centers, one of which was not far from my mom's house. She told me that she thought I would be perfect to be a Director of one of her Centers. She told me that I would need five more credit hours in Child Development and that as long as I was taking the classes, the state would allow me to be the Director of the Center. I agreed to take a couple more Child Development classes. I already had 10 credit hours in Child Development.

I enrolled for a class in Child development at Trek's Community College and was on a monthly payment plan. I took Ms. Tape the paper work to show her that I had already enrolled in a class and she was pleased. The book I needed for the class was eighty dollars. I had been back at my mom's for almost a month. When I was staying there before I would pay her rent around the first of the month. I knew I needed to pay for the book and take care of some other things that I had to take care of. I explained my situation to my mom and asked her if I could make up some of the cost next month when I paid rent the following month. She said that was fine and not to worry about it.

About a week later, I heard Tony fussing at my mom. I realized that he was complaining that I had not given my mom any money yet. I then realized that before I left the last time he must have found out from my mom that I was paying her rent. I assume that he had not known all along and something happened where it was made known. I really understood then what Tony meant when he told me that that was my home and I take care of it. When he said that I did ask myself what is he talking about. Right then I knew.

Tony was willing to let me stay because he saw dollar signs. It was all about getting some money from me and not necessarily about helping my children and I. That was okay, even though that's how it was, it still helped my children and I because we had a place to live. I went and got the money that I had and tried to give it to my mother but she would not take it so I took it and gave it to Tony. Tony took it and he shut up.

The first day of class the instructor mentioned that a copy of the book that we needed for the class was in the library and could be used while in the library. That was music to my ears and it worked out great for me. I would go to the library to read from the textbook, take notes and do homework assignments before or after class. I completed the class and was prepared to register for another on the following semester but before I could, I received a telephone call from Ms. Tape saying that she needed a teacher for one of her locations.

Ms. Tape indicated that she still wanted me to be the Director of the third center that she was opening but she needed a teacher in her second center immediately. I met with her at that center and she explained that the original teacher called in sick and she lost her job because as Ms. Tape said, she had a business to run and she did not have time for people who could not be at work. I thought that was strange because things happen, and people do get sick and I felt that room should be given for those unexpected situations. Although I thought Ms. Tape was being unreasonable, I went with it. I felt like she did not care about the employee's well being but only cared about her business.

I ended up leaving there by telling her that I needed to find child care for my daughter. I worked on getting child care and Ms. Tape and the Director of that center even told me about a place that took children my daughter's age. She was not a toddler yet and was still considered an infant. I had to think about what would be convenient for me, especially considering that I used public transportation as my form of transportation at the time.

The center that the Director told me about was not in route and would be a big inconvenience. Furthermore, I was very particular about where I would leave my child. I had to check the program out and feel that I felt that it was a good place for her. Ms. Tape was rushing me and wanted me to just put her anywhere. By the end of the week, Ms. Tape told me that the original teacher called and begged for her job back and she gave it back to her. I was okay with that. I felt like the lady should have never been fired in the first place, especially considering the reason she was fired.

I realized that I did not want to work with Ms. Tape and that all that happened to show me her true character. I forgot about being a director at her third center and I believe she did too because I never heard from her again. I was okay with the outcome. I felt like I had just dodged a bullet!

CHAPTER 25

Eventually I decided to go back to work for Gracious Home Care. I went to their office and went through the application process again. I had an interview and was given a day to come back for training. I had also enrolled in an online Masters program. I had decided to pursue a Masters Degree in Business Administration. I did not have a computer so I would go to the computer lab at Olive-Harvey Community College and use theirs. One day I went and realized that I couldn't get back into the online classroom. I believe that the employees of the lab had set the computers so that I could not get in.

One day prior to that, I noticed that one of the employees in the computer lab had looked on the computer that I was working on while assisting the person on the computer next to me. It was obvious that I was on a site of another school. That must have been an issue and the truth is that I should not have even been in their computer lab because I was no longer a student there. I got away with it because no one asked for ID. You could just walk in and that's what I did. That was put to an end.

I decided to go and use the computers at Chicago State University. Their computers did not allow me to access certain parts of my schools website, so what I could do was very limited. I figured that I would try the computers at the public library. That is what I did. The only thing was that you could only work on their computers for an hour. If someone had reserved the computers, you could not sign back in again after your hour was up. I worked with it the best way that I could and it worked out oaky.

Although Larry and I were not in an intimate relationship, we were still friends. We hung out quite a bit and we would sometimes smoked weed together. I could see how my being friendly with Larry was probably not the best thing to be doing but I continued to go along with it because I really just wanted to keep peace. I'm sure there were also some internal issues that I may have had that caused me to be somewhat dependent on that dysfunctional relationship. The fact of the matter is that I knew that this was an explosion waiting to happen and it usually did happen is some small ways whenever I decided to distance myself from Larry and avoid him. Usually when I did this he would petition me to court.

The first time he petitioned me to court was for joint custody. The second time was for joint custody where he did not have to pay child support. We both would take care of his needs when he was with us. The third time concerned me stating that I was allowing him to take Rasheed to Minnesota. Larry and his girlfriend Marcia were planning to move to Minnesota because he had a music producer there he was working with and he was going there so he could work on his music. That never took place. They did not go to Minnesota and the music was never produced.

A couple of times after that we were in court for joint custody along with special features. I'm sure that the judge knew that Larry was having a ball bringing me to court for such petty issues. The thing was that I was never tripping or giving him any problems concerning Rasheed. It was all about control. I guess that was the only way he could get me to move because he was pushing the buttons and here I thought women were the ones that used the children to play games and control their children's fathers. The roles were clearly reversed here.

This particular time was the final shebang. I had decided to tell Larry that he could pick up Rasheed on Fridays at school and drop him off at school on Mondays and I would get him from there on Fridays. Clearly I was doing this to avoid Larry. This way I did not have to see him and he could get his son. The first Friday that he was to get him from school, he came by my mom's house where I was staying. Rasheed came into the room and said, "my daddy said can I stay with you for good?" I said, "yes" and Rasheed left back out. The next thing I know is that Larry stormed in the room pushing my bedroom door open like it was his house.

He was going on and fussing and looking crazy and angry. I just stood there and watched. I did not say anything. There was nothing to say. He eventually turned around to leave the house, and as I walked behind him to lock the door he turned around to battle with me and I swung at him. See, I was tired of dealing with his controlling self, wanting to control me and playing games with my son to be ignorant. I ended up in a choke whole just about out of breath. Tony paced back and forth and I believe he was hoping that he would hurry up and kill me. My brother Demetrius came up the stairs and flipped out when he saw Larry choking me. Demetrius kept saying, "I know you do not have your hands on my sister". He eventually let me go and he and my brother were into it. My brother picked up a bat that was by the front door and swung it at Larry. Larry ran out of the door.

I was very distraught after the incident and I felt like I could not deal with the drama with Larry any more. I went in my room and got on my knees and prayed. I told God that I needed help and I needed to get out of there. I knew that Larry would always show up and cause trouble as long as he could get to where I was. I was also concerned about the fact that he did this at my mother's house. It's like he did not have any respect for her or her home. I was very happy that it was at my mom's house at the same time. Would he have choked me until I had no more life if my brother had not been there to put an end to the choking?

Whatever the case may have been, I knew I had to make a move and I had to make it fast. Sometimes you know when it's time to make a change and I knew it was time for me to do just that. All of a sudden I remembered a telephone number that a lady gave me when I was at a place applying for rental assistance. Several months prior to that day I was looking at apartments and hoping to move into my own apartment. I went to a place that I heard about that helps you pay your initial move in rent and security deposit.

While I was doing my intake interview with a staff member, a lady that was being helped by another staff member turned to me, handed me a piece of paper with a telephone number and told me that this place helps you when you are in an abusive situation. She said that they will help you get back on your feet and help you find a place. It was weird to me because I didn't think that I had said anything to indicate that I was in an abusive situation. I do remember saying that it was not a good situation and I just needed to get out of there.

I called the number and explained my situation and was routed to a Domestic Violence Shelter. I went to the shelter that evening. I brought several huge bags for my three children and myself. The bags had to be searched before they let us in. The staff showed us to our room and we got settled in. We got a decent night's sleep and when I woke up the next morning I called my mom's house. My brother told me that the police had been by there looking for me.

It seemed that Larry had went to the police station and said that I attacked him. My brother told the police that I was not there. I found out that the police came back again a couple of days later and my brother told them again, that I was not there. They gave him a card with their information for me to call them. They said that because they were unable to contact me that there would be a warrant for my arrest.

I finally called the officer and was informed that Larry said that he wanted to press charges but they had to get my side of the story. I told the officer what happened and I even pointed out that Larry was at my house when he should not have been there so it sounds more like he came to where I was for a fight, so how was it that I attacked him? The truth is that I did swing on him first and that's exactly what he wanted me to do so he could do just what he did. He wanted me to pay because I would not do what he wanted me to do. I would not let him control me and he was mad as hell!

CHAPTER 26

The shelter we were in was pretty cool. It made me think of a castle and a mansion. We had chores every day. You had to follow the rules to be able to stay in the shelter and to get the proper help and assistance needed to help you transition into independence. There were a few ladies there that had been there before me and knew the ropes. We became cool right away. It was a really nice feeling among us women. There was no drama or discord among neither of us. That was rather rare to see with several females, particularly black females, and it was cool.

I suppose that our common bond was that we were all there because we had to remove ourselves and our children from abusive situations. We had to learn how to survive outside of those situations. We had had enough and that is what brought us together. We also had to pick a day out of the week to be assigned to cook dinner for all the families in the shelter. I really enjoyed it when it was my turn to cook. Sometimes two or more of us teamed up and cooked together. There were three of us who were regulars for cooking dinner. I really enjoyed bonding with the ladies in the shelter.

One day I had to go to Rasheed's school to transfer him out. When the staff person asked me what school I was transferring him to, I did not want to say because I did not want Larry to reach us but I made the mistake of saying the school was in Tinley Park. Go figure. It wasn't hard to figure out what school he was at considering there are not many elementary schools in small suburbs. The next thing I know is that my counselor came and got me to talk. She told me that Larry had been calling the school that Rasheed was attending and had been harassing the school by telephone saying that he had custody of him and that I had kidnapped him. My counselor said that we needed to leave for our own safety. They helped me to locate another shelter. They also agreed to allow me to leave the following morning.

When I first went to the shelter in Tinley Park I found out that they had a computer lab. That was great because I was taking an online class. After I got my children in bed at night, I would go into the computer lab and do my schoolwork. The day my counselor informed me that we needed to relocate, it was my last day of the online class. I had been working on the final assignment and was planning to complete it and submit it that night. That is the reason why I asked if we could leave the following morning. That worked out great.

The following morning I left there and relocated to another shelter. There was one shelter in the Northern suburb area of Chicago I preferred to go to but they had indicated that they did not have any openings and plus it was quite a ways from where I was. I went to a shelter on the west side of Chicago. The shelter was like a midpoint between the shelter I left and the shelter I wanted to go to. One of the ladies from the shelter that I was leaving drove me there and I paid her. We agreed to keep in touch and we did for a little while.

When we got to the new shelter we were taken to our room and the rules were explained to me. I was roommates with a lady named Doris. Doris had a son named Michael. Doris and I became really good friends. We would hang out together and we spent quite a bit of time at the park near the shelter. I did not intend on staying in that shelter and so I had not registered Rasheed in school. I really did not want to register him in a public school in the city because Larry may have his old school look it up to see where he was.

Christina would catch the bus to school. She stayed at her same High School. She was a freshman and I was hoping to let her stay there until the end of the school year or at least as long as she could.

I caught the bus with her along with Rasheed and Freedom to show her how to get there. Rasheed, Freedom, and I stayed at my mom's house until Christina got out of school. We left my mom's to go back to the shelter and I explained to Christina how to get back to the shelter after school. After that Christina caught the bus on her own and I stayed at the shelter.

One day one of the staff asked me why Rasheed was not in school. I told her that he was not enrolled in school yet. She told me that I had to enroll him in school. She said that she could not have him around all day when he should be in school and she gave me some paperwork and directions to the school to enroll him the next day. I enrolled Rasheed in school the next day and found myself really bored at the shelter.

While at the shelter I noticed how militant the staff treated the ladies there. It was as if we were in prison. I felt like here we were in a situation where we left an abusive relationship and came to them for help and they were somewhat abusive too. It felt like the ladies in the shelter were being punished. Now don't get me wrong, I get that most of the women who came through those doors needed discipline and rules to follow but I think they went a little overboard. Then again I may not have been seeing the whole picture of what they may have known that I didn't know. Nonetheless, I realized that that place was definitely not for me.

The next day I called my Aunt Linda and asked her if my children and I could come to her house for about a week and then go to the shelter near her home. She agreed to let me come and said that I would have to make some kind of means to leave after a week because I could not be there long. Although I was a little shocked at her saying that, it was okay. I did not want to stay at her home. I was actually trying to get to the shelter near her home when I left the first shelter. I just made a pit stop to the second shelter because the one I wanted to go to did not have any openings and it worked out so that traveling from the first shelter to the second shelter would not be too much. The fact of the matter is that I needed to take a break from the shelters and wanted to come to her house before calling the other shelter near her house. That Saturday my aunt came and picked us up from the shelter and we went to her condo. I was in the second shelter for only one week and one day.

During the week we were at my Aunts house Christina continued to go to her same High School. Towards the end of the week I called the shelter and they told me they did not have any room right then but they would in about a week. They also said that they could put me in a motel until the spot opened up. I agreed to that and I transferred Christina out of her High School. When we got to the motel, I registered both Christina and Rasheed in a school in the suburb where we were staying at the motel and where the shelter was that we would be at when the spot was available.

Christina and Rasheed went to school from the motel for about a week. A cab came to get Rasheed to take him to school and Christina rode the public bus. The cab service was set up and paid for by the school district. The service was for children in homeless situations at the motels. I rode the bus to Christina's school the first day to show her how to get there and met her after school to show her how to get back to the motel. The school agreed to give her all of her credits if she did well the rest of the school year. It was the middle of April and she had about a month and a half at that school to go. That worked out really well. When I registered Christina, everyone was so helpful and made sure that we got everything that we needed for Christina to have a good start. It felt like we were getting special treatment and it was special. I learned so much about the funds and things that are available for homeless students. I felt like we were well taken care of.

We finally went to the shelter after about a week in the motel. The shelter looked kind of like a really big castle or a mansion. It was a lot like the first shelter except it was not as new and fresh as the first one. My children and I had our room. The residents at the shelter had chores but the staff was not as diligent about enforcing the chore rules to the women in the shelter. I did my chores and I found myself overcompensating for all of the women who did not do their chores. I cleaned the bath room by my room regularly even when it was not my chore. I felt that because my children and I used it, I wanted to make sure it was clean all the time. The women there were pretty cool. Again, bonds and friendships were formed.

CHAPTER 27

I had decided to continue the online classes and they had started right after I moved into the shelter. There were no computers for the residents to use in the shelter. I initially went to the library and took Freedom most of the time to do school work. I was doing okay but not as well as I could have. I could only use the computers for an hour and it was kind of difficult because I had Freedom with me. Freedom was two years old and she needed tending to for the most part. Eventually this became too much and I decided to withdraw from the class.

I felt that I was trying to do too much and the fact was that I was homeless. I needed to have a stable home before I could go back to school. I called to speak with my academic counselor about withdrawing. He put the enrollment counselor on the line with us. The enrollment counselor tried to convince me to stay enrolled. I told her that I was not interested in being talked into staying when I knew it was not right for me at the time. She told me that my withdrawal status at that point (2 weeks) in the class would cause me to owe the school money. I told her that I would just have to deal with that because at the time I could not perform well in class due to my situation. I withdrew from the class.

I knew that I should have not registered for the second class because of my homeless status but I felt that I could stick it out at the time. I also did not consider the fact that I would owe the school money if I withdrew from the class after only being two weeks in. Actually I was not aware that this would happen so I couldn't take it into consideration when I agreed to continue with my second class. It was too late for worrying about that. I had to do what was best and that is what I did.

It had been heavy on me to move to Minnesota. I initially tried going to Indianapolis, Indiana because it was closer. I even called the domestic violence shelters there and asked questions about how their programs worked. The thing is going to Minnesota was weighing heavy on me. I knew for sure that God was leading me to go to Minnesota. The shelter had a fund that I could apply for to pay for our travel expenses to Minnesota. I eventually applied for it and was approved for the funds. That organization paid for our tickets to get to Minnesota.

My plan was to wait until the school year ended and then leave. Before that happened, I received a message from the shelters director indicating that Larry had been calling the school district saying that he had custody of Rasheed and that I had kidnapped him. I began to call legal aid offices to get some help. The legal aid person that worked with the residents in the shelter looked up my case and found that during court Larry had been granted full custody of Rasheed.

I did not show up at court because I was afraid that I would be arrested. After learning about the warrant, I went to the court to try to resolve the problem but when I talked to the court clerk I was told that depending on what the judge decided, I could be arrested. I thought about my children and knew I could not risk possibly going to jail. I left the court that day having solved nothing. I also had a court date to take a DNA test for Freedom. I did not show up there either because I was concerned that I could get arrested. I did not know how the warrants worked with the courts and rather they would know about the warrant or what they would do if they did, so I did not want to take any chances.

After finding out that Larry had obtained full custody of Rasheed, I knew that I had to do something and that's why I called legal aid. Every legal aid office asked me for my name and Larry's name and then told me that they could not help me. One particular agency asked me for a little more information and I remember telling them that I was in Waukegan. Soon after I found out that Larry was calling the school district I realized that Larry had called all of the legal aid agencies in Cook County and no one could help me because of the conflict of interest. The one agency that asked me where I was gave that information to Larry and that is how he knew where we were and called the school district.

CHAPTER 28

Eventually I came to the realization that I had to send Rasheed with his dad. I did not want any other legal problems and definitely did not want to live like a fugitive. I knew that it would only bring me problems and I needed a clean and fresh start. God had really been dealing with me about handing Rasheed over to Larry. The situation with Abraham from the bible was impressed upon me, as to how he offered his only son to God and he did not ultimately have to give up his son because of the ram in the bush. The other impression left on me was that God gave his only begotten son for me and he gave me my son and so it would be me giving my son back to God. God was reassuring me that everything would be alright.

I ended up calling Larry's dad and asked him to come and get Rasheed. He agreed and came and got him. I had a really good talk with Rasheed about it and let him know we both had to be strong and everything would be okay. The day that Larry Sr. came to get Rasheed was a little sad. The shelter director was anticipating telling me that I had to send Rasheed with his dad. By the time she got to me he was already gone. There was a feeling of her wanting to be the one to tell me I had to hand him over to his dad, and instead I had done it on my own.

That night I eventually cried myself to sleep. I could feel that Rasheed's presence was gone. It really hurt so bad but I knew I had to go on. Things did get better as time went on but I could still feel the pain. He was my son, my only son whom I loved so much, and now he was gone.

Christina finished the school year and we took the Greyhound to Minnesota. The day before we left, one of the staff at the shelter gave me a telephone number to call to locate a domestic violence shelter in Minnesota. I was connected to a shelter that agreed that I could be admitted there as long as I called them by a certain time the day I was to arrive in Minnesota. They told me to call them when I arrived and they would send a cab to come and get us to bring us to the shelter.

When we arrived I called them and sure enough, they sent a cab for us. What great service, I thought. Again, I felt like I was getting great treatment. It really was a blessing considering all that I was going through. It was a blessing that those funds were in place to help women in domestic violence situations. I soon found out that Minnesota services were so much better than the services I received in Illinois.

When we got to the shelter in Minnesota we were taken to a room to do our intake and they checked our bags. We were then taken to our room. The shelter was really nice. Everything was new and fresh. The rooms were nice too and they had a really nice playground area. As we were getting settled in, another lady named Sharon was brought in the room. She had two children, an eleven year old girl and a two year old boy. We began to talk and realized that she had come from Chicago too. We became really cool and did a lot of things together.

I went to the welfare office and applied for assistance. I was able to get childcare for Freedom. Once Freedom started going to day care I was able to go to the Workforce Center and use their facilities to look for a job. One day my children (Christina and Freedom) and I went to Target. I decided to fill out an application on their computer while we were there. When I submitted the last part of the application, a message came on the computer screen asking that I wait for an associate to come and speak with me.

When the lady came to me she said that she thought that I should interview for a team lead position there because of my education in

Psychology. I agreed and she scheduled me for an interview. The interview turned out to be many interviews. I believe that the first interview went well but by the time I got to the second one it started to decline. Each interview had more than one person doing the interviewing and three at the most.

I would often refer to how I displayed certain leadership and other qualities in the shelter. I know they were thinking that my world did not go any further than the shelter. It was kind of funny in a sense. I kind of knew that I did not do my best. However, I was really happy about the experience, having been interviewed with two or more people multiple times. Although I did not think I would be chosen for the job, I called and inquired about the status. I was told that I was not chosen and was encouraged to apply for a position as a crew member. I really loved Target and had considered applying for a position as a crew member. The thing is that I had my children and other circumstances. Target really was not a good fit for me as far as for employment because I would have to work different hours, mornings, evenings, and weekends. That was not at all conducive for me at the time.

The truth of the matter is that I really needed to get a place to live and so I began to make that my priority. My family advocate at the shelter had taken me to see some apartments. I applied for one of them and when we tried to contact the landlord he was avoiding us. We realized that he really didn't want to rent to me because he did not feel that I had enough income. The thing is that he knew what my income was and told my family advocate that it was fine. The truth is that he was right, my income was not enough to rent any of his places. My only income was the SSI that I got for Freedom. I was just trying to get into a place and figured I would work the rest out later.

The shelter paid the application fee for me. This was another benefit of the funds that were set aside for women in domestic violence situations. We eventually let it go and the man never returned any calls to say anything. I had applied to another apartment that was a little more affordable. The shelter paid the application fee for me, and again the landlord started avoiding me. She eventually let me know that she did not think that after paying my rent that I would have enough to live on and she was right!

I began to look through a book at the shelter with different housing programs. I applied to a few that I qualified for. One of the ones I applied to was the YWCA transitional housing program. I called and was told that they did not have any openings. I was beginning to get frustrated and I was really ready to leave the shelter. The shelter was a thirty day stay shelter, and I had seen people that left after their thirty days. I was thinking that I had to find somewhere quick because my thirty days was approaching.

One day I was talking to one of the staff about it and she told me that I didn't have anything to worry about. She said that they would not make me leave because I had been taking care of my business. That told me that the ones that they made leave after their 30 days left because they were not as proactive as I was. I also believe that God was just working things out for me.

A few days after I was told that I didn't have to worry about leaving, my family advocate told me that she spoke to someone at the YWCA. She asked me if I would be interested in going there after she explained how the program worked to me. I told her that I had contacted them and they said that they did not have any openings. She said that she knew a lady that worked there who was a part of deciding who is accepted into the program. She said that the lady used to work at the shelter.

My family advocate explained that they would interview me if I was interested. I said that I was absolutely interested. Again, God was working. I went to the interview and by the time that I got back to the shelter, my family advocate told me that they had called and decided to accept me into the program. I was so happy and thankful to God, the decision makers and my family advocate. God was really working things out for us.

I had to go to the Section 8 office to get the process started. The program worked with Section 8 to pay the rent for the people in the program. It was a two year program and if you decided to leave after a year, you could but you could stay for two years if you chose to. When you leave the program and are successful at abiding by the rules and keeping out of trouble, you get to keep your Section 8. I thought that was a really good deal. The welfare offices in Minnesota are called the county office instead of the public aid office or welfare office like in Chicago, Illinois. Your county office is the office that's in the county that you live in. They help you pay rent deposits and moving expenses if you are eligible. They paid my deposit and my prorated rent for the month I moved into the YWCA transitional housing program.

CHAPTER 29

There were rules for the program. We could not have over night guest in our apartment. I had to meet with my case manager regularly and participate in the workshops and outings. It was actually a really cool program. My children and I really benefited from all the help we got since going to the shelter after the incident with Larry at my mom's house. I always felt that that incident took place to help me move forward in my life and I thank God for all the help he has given me along the way.

After being in the shelter for almost a year, I decided I wanted to move on. I followed the proper procedure to move out and I found an apartment. The apartment was in an apartment rental booklet. I had already marked the apartment complex to check it out when a lady from the program had recently moved in there, told me about it. She told me that the apartments were really nice. I went to apply and was approved. I went to the county and they agreed to pay my deposit. I had also learned that the county could also pay your moving expenses. It seemed that they did not tell you about it up front. You had to know about it and ask and so that is what I did.

They agreed to pay for a certain dollar amount for my moving fees and gave me the information for two companies to choose from. I took care of everything I needed to and had everything in place to move. On the day that we moved to our new apartment, things were really good. The movers came and moved everything in a little over an hour. Christina and I caught a cab to the new place. After we got moved in, we got some things put in order and after some time we went to pick up Freedom from day care. Freedom was enrolled at a home day care near our old place. When we came back home, I noticed a lot of noise and activity in the area. After a while, I realized that we had moved to the clean projects.

The apartment complex was recently renovated so everything was new. When I would come by there to take care of things while I was in the process of applying and doing the proper paperwork for the apartment, it would be during the day. It would be really quiet and calm then. I learned the day we moved in that it was not always quiet and calm. That was something I had no choice but to adjust to until I was able to make another move. I had moved to the clean projects. I was familiar with the ghetto but not quite like this.

Prior to moving to my new apartment I had subscribed to an online dating site called Singlenet.com. I had talked to a few guys but did not see any of them as a long term mate or a husband. There was one guy who I had spoken to that seemed pretty cool. He owned his own car repair shop and was always busy and seemed to have to literally squeeze in some time for someone else. I had remembered him after I moved and decided that I would eventually call him. Before I was able to contact him, I had received a message from this one guy. I pretty much just gave him my telephone number and told him to call me. I was at a point where I was tired of going through the process of writing messages through the web site back and forth and I felt like I could get a better feel of a person if I talked to them personally.

He called me one night really late. When I got to the telephone, I saw the name and number and realized that it seemed like it could have been him. I went back to bed and did not call the number back because I was tired and had been half sleep when he called. He called again the next day. We talked like we had known each other forever. I eventually had to get off of the phone because I had to go and get Freedom from day care. I told him that I would call him when I got back home. When I hung up the phone, I asked myself "What just happened?". I felt so connected to him and it seemed that we had known each other forever.

A little bit after I got home from getting Freedom, I called him back. His name by the way is Abraham. Abraham had been awaiting my call. We ended up talking on and off for the remainder of the evening. I found out that he lived right around the corner from Freedom's day care. We agreed that I would come by to meet him when I dropped Freedom off at day care the following morning. After I dropped Freedom off at day care the next morning, I went to the address that he gave me. I rang the door bell and after about five seconds, I started walking away. By the time that I got about twenty feet away from the door he came to the door.

I was really nervous and it showed. He came towards me and said hi. I said hello and he asked me if I wanted to come in. I said no, with an attitude. Abraham said okay and hunched his shoulders. I then asked him if I could use his restroom. He told me that I had to come in to use the restroom and we both laughed. As we walked up the stairs to get to his apartment, I said that I am using the bathroom and then leaving. Abraham directed me to the bathroom. When I got done in the rest room I went and sat down on the couch in the living room. Abraham and I began to talk and we became a little more comfortable with each other. After a little while I was ready to go and he offered to take me to my destination. I accepted his offer and that was the beginning of a developing relationship.

Abraham and I started going out on the weekends. We would go eat and he would come back to my house. Christina would be at home watching Freedom. Abraham would make sure that we brought food home for Christina and Freedom too. After dating him a couple of weeks I decided I wanted to have sex. The funny thing about it all is I had not had sex in a few years and had not planned on it until I was married. I had given my life to Christ after I gave birth to Freedom and was adamant about waiting until marriage before having sex. I had shared this piece of information with Abraham the first day I met him at his house. He initially thought it was weird and said having sex was a way of getting to know a person you're with. He then went on to say that if that's what I wanted then it was fine with him.

When I mentioned sex to him two weeks later he was a bit surprised. This particular Sunday evening we had actually kissed. I wanted more than a kiss and told him so. I told him that I needed to take care of a few things including getting Freedom ready for and in bed. I told him to come back at a later time that evening when Christina and Freedom were in bed so we could proceed. Of course he came back and yes we did proceed. Abraham was very excited and it really showed.

I talked to God about this and felt I was safe to do it. I had gotten the impression that he could be my husband and so it was okay in my estimation to have sex with him. Well actually, it was more like once I had sex with him he would become my husband, if you know what I mean. The scriptures mention that a man and a woman become one once a man enters her. I was applying this scripture to my situation and believed that at some point we would definitely have to be legally married.

CHAPTER 30

I had not had sex since I gave my life to Christ and so I was free of any attachments to any of the guys that I had sex with and in a sense was married to because they went into me. As far as I was concerned this was a new day and a fresh start and Abraham was my husband. After we had sex, we were inseparable. Abraham came over to sleep at my apartment two days during the week and on the weekend. We became really tight. He was also really good with my children. Freedom instantly took to him and he did the same with her. He was her daddy as far as she knew and it all happened so fast that I didn't have a chance to fully process what was happening at first.

Abraham worked nights. He had two jobs. He had a full time job with a janitorial company and a part time job working on his brother's janitorial contracted jobs. Monday, Wednesdays, and Fridays were the longer days at his part time job and so he would sleep at his apartment on those nights. Tuesdays and Thursdays were his earlier nights and he would come to my apartment. We had a set routine. On the weekends we would go out to the mall or stores and go out to eat. We really did more on Saturdays and took it a little easy on Sundays.

Abraham would go and take care of some business on Sundays and sometimes I would go with him. He would go and do his laundry and get his lunch for work for the week as well as grocery shop. Sometimes we would take Christina and Freedom out with us too and have a family outing. Other times Freedom would be with us and Christina would be doing her own thing. After all Christina was a teenager. Our lives were changing. Having Abraham in our life was refreshing for the most part, especially after it just being us three for some time.

Since Abraham and I were having sex I decided to get some birth control. I tried the Nova ring and when it was time for me to take it out right before my period, I could not find it. I ended up having to go to the clinic for them to locate it and pull it out. I did not take any birth control after that and soon after I found out that I was pregnant. Abraham and I had been together for about two months and I was pregnant. It was the strangest thing but it was cool too.

Things started getting really strange. I started getting paranoid about the possibility of Abraham bothering my children in sexual ways, especially Christina. There was no proof of this just a fear and a concern. When it came to men being around my girls, I was always watchful of this kind of thing. Eventually, I realized that I was tripping. Soon after that Christina's attitude had changed. She seemed to have a nasty disrespectful attitude towards me and I did not like it.

Christina kind of wanted to just do what she wanted to without me saying anything. She wanted to be loose and have free reign and I was not having it. I was not that kind of parent. Eventually it got so bad that I realized that I needed to talk to her and if need be find here somewhere else to go. I felt like she was getting older and feeling herself and things were getting worse. I realized that we could not continue to cohabitate together like this and the thing was that I was not leaving my own apartment so it would have to be her. I thought about finding her a shelter or sending her to Job Corp.

One day I sat her down to talk to her about the situation and what we needed to work toward to help her gain some independence. I saw trouble lurking and I knew that I had to do something before it got worse. While I was talking to Christina she started rolling her eyes and smacking her lips. This was not the norm and it was unacceptable behavior. My immediate reaction was to smack her but I thought about it first and refrained. I told her that we could not wait any longer and that she needed to leave now. Christina got up from the table, went in her room and started packing.

I knew that I could not just let her leave like that so I told her to let me find somewhere for her to go. She said that she would find her a place herself the next day. I told her that I would help her find a place and she refused my help. The next day she came home from school and told me that she would be going to her friend from school house. Although I did not like what was going on, I knew in my spirit that I had to let her go. I kept hearing from within that I've done all I can do for her. I had kind of seen this coming and for a while I tried to delay this.

Christina had started wanting to hang out with her friends which was not much of a problem. I was very particular about who I allowed her to hang out with, as I felt I should have been as a parent. One day prior to all of this, Christina told me that she sometimes wants to introduce me to people and she didn't because she knew that I would not approve of her hanging around certain people. I explained to her that she was probably right. I told her as her mother it is up to me to make sure that she was around people that are okay to be around and to keep her away from people who are bad for her.

Christina did not like this. As any teenager, she wanted to do what she wanted to and wanted me to be okay with it and I wasn't. She started trying to have her friends hang out at my house and she would also ask if she could bring friends home. Sometimes she would ask if she could bring male friends home so she could braid their hair. I was okay with it for the most part but what I found was that sometimes the friends that she brought home were rude and disrespectful. Some of them did not speak and others did inappropriate things, which really was not okay when you're in someone else's home. There was a lot of disrespectful behavior going on. I spoke to Christina about it a couple of times and of course she did not like it. She pretty much just wanted me to just shut up and let her do whatever she wanted to do. Overall, it appeared that she wanted to take over my house and I was not having it.

When we were in the last shelter before we came to Minnesota, Christina met a young man at her school. They became really close.

I met him and he seemed to be a decent young man and I was okay with her relationship with him. Around the Christmas holiday, Christina asked me if he could come and stay with us for a few days after Christmas during the Holiday break. After thinking about it, I told her that was okay. I also talked with her about how things would be, what was allowed and what was not allowed. I figured it would be okay. He lived in another state and he would only be there for a few days, I didn't think it was a big deal.

He did come and everything went rather well. After he left, I started noticing different behaviors in Christina. I guess I should not have been surprised. After all, she was a teenager. I did not know how her friend coming to visit would affect her. I didn't know it until after it happened. Along with that I had just recently started dating Abraham and our relationship became close and serious swiftly. All of this was affecting Christina in a way where she wanted what I was having with Abraham. In other words she wanted to be grown and in a relationship.

All of these events are what ultimately led to her having to relocate. It had gotten completely out of hand and she had gotten very rude and disrespectful. In fact, the day that I sat her down to talk to her about finding her somewhere else to live and she was rolling her eyes and smacking her lips, I wanted to smack her and my inner guide helped me to refrain from smacking her. My inner voice said that she may call the police on me if I smacked her. I realized that it was not worth the drama and I definitely was not trying to have any encounters with the law. After all, I still had Freedom to look after. What I knew for sure was that someone had to go and it was my apartment and I was the adult and so it definitely would not be me.

CHAPTER 31

Christina stayed at a friend's house. She kept in touch and I was glad she did because I was still concerned for her and I wanted to make sure she was okay. It felt so strange to be in that situation with Christina but I knew it was best for both of us. There was also a concern of how it looked to others. Overall, I could not really concern myself too much about that because I knew that I was doing what I felt was the best thing to do, although it was not easy.

Christina had some things at my apartment and would still come by sometimes to get things. She eventually told me that she was moving to another friend's house. One day I received a telephone call from a lady named Elaine. Elaine said that she was Yolanda's mom. Yolanda was the friend that Christina said she was moving with. Her mom wanted to know if it was okay with me for her to stay there. I told her it was fine and that Christina had been gone from my house for a while.

It seemed that Christina had given Elaine the impression that I was giving her permission to move with her as if she was still in my care. I kind of appreciated Elaine for calling me and asking me if it was okay for Christina to move in her home. I thought it was a little strange that the parents of the first friend she stayed with did not call and see what was going on. As a parent and adult myself, if my daughter came to me asking me if her friend could come and live with us, I would want to speak to her parents.

Prior to Christina leaving, I discovered that I was pregnant. I had not decided on another form of birth control after my doctor got the nova ring out and I did not see another period either. Talk about a fast moving relationship. Abraham was excited about the pregnancy. It was a cool thing in a way. He went the extra mile to make sure I had the things that I needed. I really loved him for that and I appreciated the way he cared for me. He also cared for Freedom as if she were his own. He made attempts with Christina too. He was a blessing.

Before Christina left I had planned a trip for Christina, Freedom and myself to take the Greyhound bus to Chicago. Since it was already planned, I told Christina that she could still go. She met me at the Greyhound Station and we went to Chicago together. We stayed at my mom's house. I had not mentioned that I was pregnant to anyone except my mom. I was only about three months at the time. We stayed there for four days and went back to Minnesota. When we got back to the Greyhound Station in Minnesota, Christina said that she would be catching a bus to her friend's house. My mother was the only one in Chicago who knew that Christina was no longer in my care. We managed to get through the entire visit without it being mentioned. It's not so much that it was a secret but it was not anyone's business. At that point it was a private matter which we were getting used to and working through ourselves. It was still fresh and we definitely did not need the stress of third parties having their input or having to explain and deal with others opinions about a matter that was already fragile and emotional for us.

Christina continued to go to school and she had even gotten a job at one time. She could not continue to work because the job was really far and not on a bus line that had late bus service. The job required that she work late some days and she could not because of a lack of transportation, so she had to let the job go. I was proud of her for trying. I liked the idea that she was determined to keep pressing on and make a decent life for herself.

In all actuality, her leaving my house was good for her in this sense. Christina wanted to lean on me too much. She was getting older and growing into a young adult. I had sheltered her so much because I did not want her to be subjected to the things I went through as a child. I also just wanted to protect her from the wiles of the world. I had made Christina too dependent on me, not by choice but by default. Although she did make attempts to find a job, I could not help but notice that she was also looking to me to take care of her. I did not have a problem with taking care of her basic needs but as a growing young lady she needed to have some independence and responsibilities.

On top of all of that, all the partying and hanging out she wanted to do would be at my expense. That really made things more difficult along with the fact that she resorted to trying to deal with me as if we were equals. She wanted us to be friends and I was her mother. Although I had a rather friendly relationship with her, there were boundaries and it was understood that I was her mother and that was respected. When she wanted to change all of that and have me as her peer and have me sponsor her activities, that was a sure indication that things were getting way out of control.

CHAPTER 32

I had been referred to a special OB Gyne that specialized in caring for complicated or high risk pregnancies. After having Freedom three months early, I was told that my pelvic and uterus were weak. Christina was also born early and Rasheed was full term. I had some abortions and miscarriages over the years too. With my history of miscarriages and premature deliveries, my original midwife concluded that I needed a doctor that could keep a close eye on me and my pregnancy.

I had to go see the doctor every week and I had an ultrasound every two weeks. I also had to take a progesterone shot once a week. My progesterone was low and it was needed to help give the baby what it needed to stay in my wound as long as possible. Unfortunately, that was not enough. One Saturday we went to the zoo and I did quite a bit of walking. My panties were feeling wet and I noticed that I had fluids in my underwear. Later that evening when I went to the restroom it was still leakage. I decided that it was no big deal although I was a little concerned.

Abraham and I had sex that night and when I woke up the next morning I did not feel right. It felt like there was a bubble in my vagina and it was really uncomfortable. There was also more leakage than the night before. I told Abraham that I needed to go to the hospital. I called my clinic and explained the situation and they directed me to go to the hospital and go to the labor and delivery ward to be seen.

Abraham and I went to the hospital. The doctor examined me and said that the baby was sitting in my pelvic area. He said that they could try to push him back up and attempt to prolong my pregnancy but they had to run some test to see if there was some infection. When the test results came back they showed that there was some infection. The infection was dangerous for me and the baby and he said that they needed to induce my labor for me to deliver him.

The problem was that I was only twenty weeks along and the baby could not survive outside of my wound at that young age. That was their take on it anyway. I prolonged the process for a while because I had an assignment that needed to be completed. At the time I was working on my MBA and taking online classes. I actually had a meeting with my group for a project and I wanted to meet with them and let them know what was going on.

The hospital staff allowed me to take that time before they induced my labor. In the meantime Abraham went to my house to get Freedom off of her school bus. I had made arrangements for him to take her to my friend's house for the night. I went back and forth in my mind as to whether I should let them induce my labor. I called Abraham and told him that I probably could hold the baby inside of me as long as I could and maybe he could survive in my womb for a while longer. The doctor had indicated that it was up to me but he did let me know it was risky for the baby and myself. They also said that if I decided to do that, I would need to be on bed rest.

I was trying to be optimistic and believe that God would work it out and I could pull it off. Then I called Abraham to see what he thought. Abraham said that he did not think that it was a good idea. He felt that I would be risking my own life too. I decided to proceed and have my labor induced. By the time Abraham got to the hospital, I had already delivered Peace.

I held Peace and did not want to let him go. I was discharged the next day and before I left, I held Peace and rocked him although he was no longer alive. The nurse noticed how I did not want to let him go and she told me that she was so sorry. Eventually I let go and when Abraham came to get me we went home. We went to pick up Freedom first. The ride home was very quiet. Abraham and I were at a lost for words. When we got to my apartment he seemed to not know what to say to me. All we could do was look at each other. We were feeling very close to one another, yet we did not know how to console one another.

Abraham had missed work at his full time job the day before and it did not make sense for him to miss another day. I told him that I was okay and that he could go to work. There was not much that could be done at that point and I needed to have some time to myself. I knew that I had to keep going on and that it was just one of those things. I was okay for the most part but at the same time I was hurting over the situation. I had had miscarriages before but this was different. I actually gave birth and held Peace in my arms even when he was no longer alive. I really had a hard time letting go of him.

In the state of Minnesota when a child is born twenty weeks or after, it is considered a real birth and the child is issued a birth certificate. We had to make proper arrangements for putting the child to rest. Abraham and I did not have the money to bury Peace so we decided to have him cremated. I thought about it for a while and consulted with God about the matter. I remember a quiet voice within me saying, "from dust you came and to dust you will return". I took this as an okay to cremate Peace and that is what I did.

Although Peace had been cremated and time was passing, I still had a hard time letting go. The hospital had given me a gift box with some items and we had also taken some pictures with Peace in the hospital. I decided that the only way to move on from this was to truly let all of the sentimental things about him go. One day I took the box and all of its contents along with his pictures and his remains to the lake and pitched them in the lake. That is how I finally said good bye.

CHAPTER 33

Abraham and I were at a very different place in our relationship. The experience with Peace seemed to have brought us closer. Although we were close we seemed to start to argue more. A lot of my issues began to surface. I became a bit abusive. I would have moments of rage where I would physically attack him because of something that was happening that I did not like, agree with or felt that it was disrespectful.

I felt like an abusive woman toward my man and although I did not like my behavior I felt that I had no control over it. At that time, attacking physically and verbally were the only ways I knew how to relieve my frustration until this one particular day. Abraham was driving his car while I sat in the passenger seat and Freedom sat in her car seat in the back seat and I went into one of my rages. I started punching Abraham in the face and he initially tried to restrain me and resorted to punching me on the side of my arm several times to stop me. He then stopped the car and tried to open my door and push me out of the car.

I calmed down because I did not want to get out of the car. Abraham had had enough and although I don't condone a man hitting a woman it was just enough for me to get a hold of myself and my erratic behavior. I especially noticed how he was trying to get me out of the car while my daughter was still in the car. I guess he felt that Freedom was not the problem but I was, and I was. Abraham was very meek and did not do anything to prompt my behavior. The things that I would try to fight with him about were not because of things that he was doing that were not right but rather my perception of them because of my tainted lenses and emotional baggage. I am not saying that Abraham was perfect but her did not deserve or do anything for me to behave that way. I had serious issues and I knew I had to do something about them.

Things got better with Abraham and I, or should I say I got better and learned to control myself. In fact, I began to delve deep into helping myself be a better more whole person. I read books, many books. I read a lot of spiritual books emphasizing Christian principles as well as new age and metaphysical literature. I even started looking at Buddhism and Muslim literature. Self help books were a must for me and I learned and read about many subjects from how the brain functions to psychological literature to taking care of your soul and spirit. I looked at literature surrounding relationships too. I even went to see a therapist from time to time.

As I was learning more about myself, human behavior, and spiritually, I was determined to have Abraham on the same page as myself. After Abraham and I finally married after being in an intimate relationship for almost two years, I felt that things would start to fall into place. Boy was I in for a surprise. I went through a long period of trying to get Abraham to see things my way according to all of the awareness that I was coming into.

Abraham and I would argue and I would be so frustrated about him not cooperating with all that I was trying to show him, including how he needed to change. Part of my reason for being so determined to get him right was because of my awareness that God wanted to use me to help him grow spiritually and then financially. I knew I had to grow up first to help him grow up. The only problem was that I was going about it all the wrong way.

After being exhausted and very frustrated with my attempts of getting Abraham to know what I was learning and then act accordingly, I got an epiphany. I learned that I needed to just make the changes in my life and lead by example and he would change on his own in his own time. Furthermore, I learned that it should not be my motive to change him or make him change. I realized that I needed to focus on myself and pay attention to what was happening with my inner man, to get to the root of the problem and implement some resolutions.

Things were getting better but on the other hand they were getting worse. As I began to grow up and change my behaviors, it seemed that Abraham would do things to get the old reactions from me. He complained about the way I had been and now that I had redirected my behavior he felt threatened by my growth. I learned that the changes I was making in my life represented the changes he was failing to make in his life. In his mind, my growth represented his demise when the truth was the opposite of that. My growth really represented the opportunity for him to grow and it gave him permission to do so but the problem was that his ego became an issue. His ego had convinced him that he could not follow my lead because he was the man I should follow his lead.

The problem was that Abraham did not have any interest in internal or spiritual growth. He was only concerned about making more money and doing something in life to make him feel better about himself. He felt that accomplishments would make him better and he failed to realize that internal growth is the key to external success. I must admit that what Abraham was experiencing was familiar to me. I too had tried to do things and have accomplishments to make myself feel better but the thing with me was I was also always on a spiritual journey, knowingly.

I was always seeking better ways, truth, and any tools that I felt would help me to be as God created me to be. Doing this eventually led me to information that caused me to see things from a different perspective, even though I did not consciously know what I was looking for. My soul knew and I would just do my best to cooperate with the unfolding and the process of my journey. You would think that I had my hands full and you would be right.

CHAPTER 34

Abraham's family members tried different tactics and manipulations to get negative reactions from me and to run me off. From the very beginning I noticed his brother's wife's attempts to aggravate and insult me. What I also learned very early in our relationship was that people wanted to use Abraham and pretty much control him. I believe that to some extent they had been somewhat successful, until I came on the scene.

Abraham's brother's wife Lucy would play little mind games with me and do underhanded things to attack me. At first I would mention it to Abraham but he would argue with me and say that I was crazy and tripping, and indicate that my claims had no legitimacy. In the beginning of our relationship I would go to parties and gatherings that his people had. Abraham is of the African descent and when I would go to gatherings that his people had, I would experience a lot of crazy looks and underhanded attacks. I mentioned this to Abraham as well and again he said that I was tripping. After a while I would notice that his brother would do things to cause a tear in our relationship. I never said anything to him about his brother. By that time I knew that he would only make me out to be crazy.

About one and a half years into our relationship Abraham's niece, Sonya came from Africa. Sonya was twenty one years old and she came to stay with Abraham's brother Josh and his wife Lucy. Very early, I noticed something devilish in her and sure enough within time it was revealed to me that she was demon possessed. Sonya's sister on her dads side, Bella came to Africa almost a year after Sonya came. She too lived with Josh and Lucy.

Josh and Lucy owned a two flat building across the street from their house. They would rent the apartments out. In fact, Abraham was living on the second floor, one bedroom apartment when I met him and soon after he moved to the first floor, three bedroom apartment with two roommates. After Bella had been in the United States for a couple of months, Lucy decided that Sonya and Bella needed to move out of her house and into the one bedroom apartment across the street. They were both working at a hair braiding shop where Josh knew the owners. The owners had first agreed to let Sonya work there and then Bella when she came.

It seemed that things would be great for Sonya and Bella but there were signs of disaster ahead. Abraham was very helpful to Sonya when she came to the United States and then to both Sonya and Bella when Bella came to the United States. He would take them to do their grocery shopping on Sundays when he went out to do his own shopping and run his errands. Sometimes people notice how helpful you are to them and they want more from you and that's exactly what happened with them.

Bella was a lot more bolder than Sonya was and she was the person in the forefront of working to get more out of Abraham. The problem was that I was in the way. One Sunday Abraham brought Sonya and Bella to our apartment for Bella to use our computer. When she came in she sat on the loveseat and cocked her legs up on the couch like she owned the place. I thought it was really interesting. I guess she assumed everything belonged to Abraham and she was all about taking over and running him. The thing was that the couch that she cocked her legs up on belonged to me and so did many other things in the apartment. In fact, the apartment was mines too. I shared it with Abraham but his name was not on anything.

Not only was Bella looking at a picture and thought she could manipulate and conquer Abraham without knowing what was really going on but Sonya was doing the same thing. Sonya was just more subtle with hers. The thing that really tripped me out was the fact that these young ladies came to a foreign country not knowing very much about it and did not waste any time trying to divide and conquer. What a way to go.

It wasn't very long until Bella began to try to control Sonya. She started torturing her too because Sonya was resisting being under her control. Sonya had mentioned to Abraham that there was a hair braiding shop in Chicago where her friend worked at. She indicated that she could go and work there but she just needed help to get an apartment. Her friend in Chicago had been a good friend of hers when she came to Minnesota. She met her at the hair braiding shop where they worked at together in Minnesota and they became really tight. Her friend had started having some troubles in Minnesota and fled to Chicago. Now Sonya wanted to flee to Chicago too to get away from her troubles with Bella.

Abraham heard Sonya's plea for help and took it all into consideration. Before Abraham could speak to Sonya about it and whether or not he would help her she called and said that she had packed up her things and left and was on the Greyhound bus to Chicago. I guess she figured that once she was already on her way, Abraham had no choice but to help her and sure enough he did. Abraham did have a choice and I'm sure he was going to help her but this way she felt it would push him to. That was the beginning of many manipulative behaviors that would occur to get what she wanted from him.

CHAPTER 35

Abraham and I were in a decent place in our relationship but that was starting to take a turn for the worse or for the better depending on how you look at it. Abraham was giving Sonya a lot of care and attention and for the most part I understood and knew that he had to help her so she could be okay. After all, we all need help from time to time in this journey called life. The thing is that for her it was all the time as if she were his responsibility. They had a relationship that was starting to look like they were girlfriend and boyfriend and that started to make my adrenaline rise.

Along with that, I could see these manipulative behaviors with her and when I would try to discuss my concerns with Abraham concerning their too close for comfort relationship, and how I saw that she wanted more from him, he would get on the defensive and say that was not the case and the end result was that I was crazy. We had a few of these kinds of discussions on different occasions and they always turned out the same, almost the same anyway. The last discussion we had, he explained his disposition and where he was coming from concerning her and her situation. He pretty much said that he was trying to be a father figure to her and give her guidance.

I told him that although he may be coming from a place of being concerned and trying to help her along her way, she seemed to be attracted to him because of it. I told him how it happens a lot, especially when young ladies did not get that kind of love and affection from their own father. I told him that he was giving her something that she never got from her father or anyone else and now that she was getting that from him, it was being distorted into an intimate attraction. Abraham insisted that that was not what she was thinking or doing. Although he said that was not what was going on, I know that it was what was going on. I figured he either did not see it or just did not want to admit that that is what it was. I left it alone and tried to just take on the perspective that although Sonya was on something inappropriate, Abraham was not and that's all that mattered.

I put my focus into myself, I tried to anyway. At that time I was in school. I was working on my Doctorate Degree in Business Administration. The online courses gave me flexibility and allowed me to work my own schedule. I had completed all of my course work and had passed the comprehension exam. I had finally made it to the final part of the Doctorate Degree Program, the Dissertation.

The Dissertation consisted of a research project where actual research had to be conducted with real people as well as documented research. In other words I had to conduct a study with people and report the findings and results. I had never done this before and people don't usually have experience in writing a Dissertation until they are at the last stages of a Doctoral Degree Program. The good thing is that the course work helps to prepare you for the work that has to be done to effectively complete a Dissertation. Committee members are also assigned to you to help you through the process and to determine whether your work is up to part. When your committee members feel that your document is up to part you have to defend your Dissertation to them and they decide whether or not you pass on. Defend really just means to present and persuade your work effectively.

During that period while working on my Dissertation I always was focused on inner growth. I've always had a fascination with human behavior, which is mainly why I majored in Psychology as an undergraduate. I was always drawn to spirituality as well. I've also always had a curious mind and wanted to understand things at a much deeper level and in some ways I always already did internally but it had to be brought out where I could understand it intellectually. I say that because when I would come into something new or learn a new way of thinking or seeing a thing on a higher level, it's always been where I felt like I knew that all along and had just remembered.

I continued to grow and mature and as my thinking began to change my behavior was changing too. As this was happening, I started to notice how my husband Abraham was uncomfortable with the changes in me. Things that he complained about concerning me were no longer an issue. The weird thing was that it seemed that he would create a situation to cause me to behave in a way that I used to before the change, just so he could complain. For example, I was really insecure about our relationship and I had trust issues at one time. He would complain about my lack of trust for him when I would question him about things that did not look right to me. After the change settled in me, I was no longer insecure about our relationship because I became more secure in myself (and God) and I put my focus and attention elsewhere.

CHAPTER 36

Abraham wanted me to be where I was again so that he could complain about me and feel better about himself. I realized that my changed represented to him his lack of change and instead of doing what he needed to do to grow himself he would rather just bring me back to where I was. I later learned that this was all unconscious feelings and behavior that he was acting out. That was very challenging for me especially considering that I knew what was going on. I did not allow this to cause me to revert backwards, as I was committed to forward movement.

I've had several experiences like this with different people. It always looks the same with slight differences. I had become accustomed to this kind of behavior and realized and learned that this was part of what comes with growth. Sometimes when you are growing and the people around you are not growing, it causes friction. As I stated before, your growth represents another's lack of growth and this just compels them to try to pull you back down so that they can feel better about themselves. In their unconscious minds this is also an attempt to keep you where you are so that they won't have to do anything to change and grow.

In my experiences I have also seen where people are not willing to do what is necessary to grow. To grow you have to take a good look at yourself and be honest about things that need to change. Many people do not want to have to do anything to change. They just want things to change for them, for the better. When these kinds of people see someone else who's actually doing the inner work and its working for them, they resent the ones who are doing the inner work and then make attempts to diminish their progress and/or pull them backwards.

Now, all while going through this with Abraham and working on my own inner growth, I had Freedom to care for. Freedom has special needs and had been diagnosed with ADHD and eventually autism. It was up to me to make sure Freedom got what she needed to help her development. With everything going on around me I had to be very careful to make sure that the environment in our home was conducive for her growth which meant that I had to be very careful of how I handled everything. I refused to subject her to nonsense and have her in a tense environment.

This kept me constantly growing and learning new ways to deal with the unpleasant circumstances in a peaceful way and sometimes it wasn't easy or peaceful. The good thing was that I was aware of all of this and would work to recreate the peace when the peace had been lost. It got better as time went on, mainly because I started to enjoy peace over chaos. I liked peace so much that when I went out of my peaceful place, I did not feel right and so I was eager to return there.

I have to say that it took some time for me to like peace and want to keep it. I say this because like Abraham (and so many others), although I complained and fussed about things, I actually was addicted to the drama. When there was no drama, things were too boring and I would subconsciously create drama for the excitement. I actually came across some information through some of my readings that identified this in me. Once I learned about this and realized that I was doing this I worked to resolve the conflict within myself that caused this undesirable behavior.

Sonya and Abraham were still doing what they do and I had for the most part gotten over it. It really didn't bother me anymore and I had decided that was them and what they do, and I needed to stay focused on my inner growth and advancement. Sonya would still do little underhanded things to get a negative reaction out of me mainly because she had witnessed an argument between Abraham and I the summer that she first came to the United States. She wanted to continue to get that reaction from me and ultimately wanted it to cause a separation between Abraham and I.

I would have dreams that showed me what she was contemplating and plotting. At one point of time she actually wanted to have a sexual relationship with him. I believe she made very subtle attempts to entice him but he was unresponsive. In fact, there were times that Abraham would share things with me concerning her and I would be able to see what she was really on. I actually was able to see this concerning a lot of things. I have to say there were a couple of instances where I did react to her and pretty much told her about herself. One time in particular I was led to apologize afterwards. The fact was that no matter what she was doing, I needed to handle myself a certain way and I had failed to, so I had to apologize for the way I spoke to her.

It still did not stop there. There was a combination of her trying to aggravate me and at other times she would try to be of interest to me so that I would want to befriend her. The truth is that I had no interest in befriending her. I was not her peer and she was confused about that in some ways. Abraham did not help with this, in fact he contributed to her being this way because he handled her like they were friends and as I said before, to the point where they looked like a couple.

I had experienced this with my own daughter Christina in the way that I was friendly with her and she had a hard time with the boundaries of respect and I realized that I had played a part in that. When I saw it and attempted to shift my way of relating to her, she didn't like that and it became chaotic. I was able to see what was going on with Abraham and Sonya and part of it was due to my own experience with Christina.

Here and there I would mention things to Abraham that concerned me about their relationship but he always had a defense or an excuse. Eventually I came into the knowledge and understanding that they were emotionally bonded. They provided something for one another. Sonya was needy and Abraham needed to be needed.

Remember, I was growing up and was a lot more self-sufficient and aware, so I was not needy anymore. I was never as needy as Sonya was but had some needy behaviors when it came to Abraham and our relationship until I changed my mind and behavior.

CHAPTER 37

I was becoming more and more conscious of myself and had read quite a bit of material that led me to greater awareness and consciousness. Now just because I had a greater awareness than I had before does not mean things around me were easier. As they say, "practice makes perfect". Things would calm down for a while and before you knew it there was more drama. The good thing about it is that I realized that it was good for me. I was exercising my muscles. I was getting stronger and flexible. I was in training, training for something great. I had to master the challenges before me to past on to the next phase of my life.

Something great was in store for me. I knew it then, like I always knew it. The difference was that I was more in touch with it than before and closer to it too! I became more entrenched with my spiritual studies. As I would apply spiritual principles, more drama would appear. This was what I learned to be spiritual warfare. I did get breaks here and there but just before you knew it, here we go again, and so that was the cycle. It was like an emotional roller coaster. Heck, it was an emotional roller coaster.

Eventually I realized that I needed to deal with myself from an emotional stand point. I further realized my emotional defects after learning that I was an emotional eater. I had gone to the clinic one day because I had stomach pain. I found out during that visit that my blood pressure was really high. The doctor who's care I was in at the time kept a close watch on me and ran some test. I ended up having to take medication to help lower and control my blood pressure.

During that period my doctor and I discussed the importance of weight loss for my circumstances. I was almost 100 pounds overweight. According to what the medical and nutritional experts call BMI index. During our discussion I mentioned that I tend to eat when I am having an emotional situation going on and that is just about all the time. I told her that I realized that I needed to work through childhood issues and so I was going to see a therapist.

I had learned that many times we respond to present situations or events in our life as if it was something familiar from our past, when it isn't our past. In other words we can live in our past instead of in our present and respond to the present things according to our past instead of what's really happening at the time. Anyway, my doctor told me that would be a good idea and she told me about Overeaters Anonymous (OA). She said it was like alcoholics anonymous except it was for people with eating disorders. I looked it up and started going to the meetings. I also found a therapist and started seeing her regularly. This was the beginning to a whole new chapter of this life of mine.

I continued going to the OA meetings and therapy for about four months. The OA meetings were one hour and fifteen minutes long. I liked the fellowship that came with several individuals gathered together with common issues. It was a safe haven. It felt right. One lady told me that I was home after the first meeting that I attended. I believed her. I felt God through her and I knew that God was talking to me through her.

Therapy was going well too. My new therapist's name was Dr. Escroll. Dr. Escroll was a caucasian woman, fairly tall and thin probably in her mid thirties. She was very professional and I liked that. Dr. Escroll was very attentive to my needs and she did a great job of helping me to work through my issues. I had used only about two sessions to even mention childhood issues. I found that I just needed to talk about some things that had happened and express how it made me feel.

I went on the express how I felt about it at that time. I feel that I was already past those past events but I just needed to let it out of me and release it in order to redirect some of my behaviors. I believe that I was dealing with present situations based on how I felt about things from my past that felt the same way. This contributed to my emotional eating. Although, I knew that the past was over and I didn't need to treat the present as something of my past, deep within I knew I had to release those old feelings in a safe way and in a safe place. As I began to talk about the unpleasant past events, I realized that the little girl in me just needed to be heard and understood. She needed to know that her feelings were validated. It was as if the whole part of me needed help to heal the little girl in me so that we could be whole together.

One day while I was in therapy, Dr. Escroll suggested that we try a different approach to my therapy if it was okay with me. She asked me if I felt the need to continue coming to see her every two weeks because I could just call her just to check in or come in as needed. I told her that I would come for one more appointment in two weeks then I could call her or make an appointment to see her as I felt I needed to. She seemed to think that I had done well and did not need as much therapy as I initially needed.

I believe that I was also starting to get off into areas way above her expertise. They were spiritual matters and that was not what I was there to see her about neither did we have a basis for spiritual matters throughout the therapy sessions. Either way, I realized that it was time for me to move on. I did schedule one more appointment with her but I ended up canceling it after realizing that it was not necessarily necessary, plus I was preparing to defend my Dissertation on the same day of my appointment. I decided that I needed to focus on my Final Defense for my Dissertation instead. I cancelled that appointment and did not reschedule. Meanwhile, I was starting to get the same sense at OA. I was starting to realize that OA no longer served me and so I eventually stopped going to the meetings. I continued to do self therapy and continued on my spiritual journey as I always will.

I was really nervous on the day of my Dissertation defense. Although I was nervous, I told myself to relax and be calm, they are only people and I will do great. I proceeded with my Dissertation and even I knew that I was not defending quite up to part. I read most of my material. When I was done my committee asked me some questions and I answered them. They then told me to get off of the telephone and call back in five minutes. I called back in five minutes and I was told that I answered the questions really well and my Dissertation document itself was excellent and well written but during my defense it sounded like I was reading and just going on and on.

My Dissertation chairman said that he knew all of the hard work that I had been putting into this and again my Dissertation itself was excellent but he said that I needed to improve my public speaking skills. He indicated that a lot of doing business involves giving presentations and because I wanted to own several businesses of my own, I would be doing a lot of presentations so I needed to prepare for that. I was so happy that they passed me and my chairman was absolutely correct. I knew before he said it. I needed to improve my public speaking skills and so I believe I needed him to say that to reinforce the importance for me to improve in that area.

I had prayed that my Dissertation committee would see my Dissertation as excellent, up to their standards and well put together. I prayed that my Dissertation would prove that I knew how to do the work that is required to be a Doctor of Business Administration. My prayer was answered. They said my actual Dissertation document was flawless but my presentation wasn't the best. I guess I should have prayed for a flawless presentation as well but I didn't think of that. It's okay though, I will be ready when it is time to do business.

CHAPTER 38

I scheduled an appointment with a Bariatric Clinic. I went to an information session back in the summer and had recently felt led to have a surgery so that I could have the needed assistance (smaller stomach) to lose weight and keep it off. I was thirty nine years old and forty years old was right around the corner and I was ready to be healthy. I knew I needed help and the idea of having a smaller stomach was perfect for me. See, I believed that I had a really big, out of shape stomach. When I ate, I had a lot to fill up and I did exactly that. This meant that I took in a lot of calories. Therefore, with a smaller stomach, I would only be able to eat so much because my stomach would only be able to hold so much. This meant less calorie intake and weight loss.

I went through the process and made it to the point of scheduling for surgery. I had surgery and lost weight swiftly, to the point that I had to slow it down because I did not want it all gone in a few months. I wanted it to fall off over the course of a year as it was supposed to. I would bump up my carbohydrate intake when I felt that I needed to level my weight loss off or slow it down some. I would also indulge in some junk food from time to time.

I had a plan, and originally the plan was to recover from surgery which I had in August and once Freedom was back in school in September, I would begin to look for a job. I did exactly as I planned. I began a job search after Freedom went back to school. I found that most jobs that were on the level of my education (Doctorate and Master) required quite a bit of experience in the area, which I did not have. I began to look at lower level job opportunities and found that the money was not enough in some cases. After posting my resume on Montser.com, I started receiving offers from Insurance Agencies to be an insurance agent. I actually liked the whole idea and thought that there was good money to be made working in that field.

The thing was that I would have to pay for training, tests and licensing. This was not really a big deal especially considering the opportunity for making a lucrative income. The issue was that the money was not there. I thought about how I could make it work by cutting into expenses but it seemed too risky. I needed to be able to maintain my part of our upkeep for our household while also starting a new career. The other issue was that the position was based on commission which was okay for me too but again, I needed to be able to maintain my responsibilities for the household and my daughter.

The problem was that if I used the money to pay for the expenses for training and licensing, I would not be able to keep up with my household expenses. On top of that I wouldn't be getting paid for a little while because I had to earn money which could take about a month to receive. I could not go that long without paying the bills I was responsible for, and Abraham was not in a position to help me or take over all the bills until I could make some money. I was actually offered an opportunity to work with a couple of companies. The first company was a great opportunity because of the company itself, what they offered, and how reputable they were but I did not have peace about working with the employer that was recruiting me.

The second company was a little further away from home but their expenses to get licensed were much less than the first company. I liked that and began the process. Soon I realized that they were very unorganized and lacked good management and clear communication. After several experiences with them that were very inappropriate and unprofessional on their part, I decided that that was not the place for me. The funny thing is that I kept seeing things that were not okay or very weird but I just wanted to work and produce so I looked past the craziness and tried to go on.

It just reached a point that I knew from within that I did not have to continue with this and in fact I could do so much better. I let them know that I would not be continuing with their process for getting trained and licensed to work with their company. I left a message at the telephone number that I had which went to the receptionist and I indicated that due to the circumstances I would not be returning or continuing the process. To my surprise, the receptionist called me back and left a message. She explained that due to her leaving early the day I completed the initial registration, she could not spend the time with me that was needed to explain everything correctly.

That was one of the most asinine excuses I had ever heard. I felt that it was her responsibility to explain the things that were not explained and if she left early the day she was supposed to, she should have remembered that she needed to get back to me and explain. Without going into too much detail about this, I was getting drained just from the interactions in that experience. I knew that this was just how they operated and in order for me to work in that environment I would have to fix everything or work in the midst of bad management. Either way I would have been drained and who was I to come there and get everything straight. They were not hiring me to get their office in order anyway. I was not willing to put myself through that and decided to go back to the drawing board.

I ended up remembering an email I had received from another insurance company to call for an interview. I called and scheduled an interview. I had a feeling that this company paid for the training and licensing and sure enough they did. This company was very careful about the individuals they selected to go on to more interviews for possible selection into their company as an agent or a management position. The company was growing and expanding and so they were recruiting people for different positions.

This job entailed that employees work evenings and weekends and although I was not too happy about that I was willing to try it if I were selected. The compensation for the jobs was unreal and that motivated me to adjust to any changes in scheduling as needed. I was also just ready to work and produce and so I was just about willing to accept any opportunity that allowed me to make a substantial income. While I was in the company's office for an interview, an information session with other candidates, and then another interview, it felt a little weird.

There was a vague feeling of uneasiness when I was there. The regional manager spoke during the information session and there was something about him that was familiar but I could not put my finger on it. To tell you the truth, I was not even trying to, but I noticed something familiar and off. I was so busy trying to hear about the opportunity and see if I fit into what they were offering that I tried to not see things that were not so pleasant. I was kind of just going with the flow and hoping for the best.

After not hearing back from them that evening, I felt that they were not going to call me back for a third interview. Eventually, it was revealed to me that the company was just like the company in the movie "The Devil's Advocate". When I really thought about it the speaker in the information session reminded me of Al Pacino in The Devil's Advocate. The company was driven by the same spirits as the ones in The Devil's Advocate. It was a spirit of greed and cocky pride and I could not be a part of that no matter how much money I could make. I felt that the interviewers and the speaker knew that I would not go along with it and so they did not consider me as a possible candidate for any of their positions.

I must say that they were absolutely correct. I would not have gone along with their way of doing things. Although I was aware of the situation at this company, I still had a little bit of a hard time letting go. The compensation for working with the company was great. For starters it could have been between four thousand to six thousand dollars a month. That was a big deal to me at the time. I was so motivated about making money that I still hoped that they might call me. Those figures stayed with me for some time. Also, I kept receiving emails from them to call to schedule an interview but it was like the one I had already done.

After receiving so many emails from them I read the bottom of the email that indicated that I would continue to receive emails from them because I was on their mailing list. I felt led to contact them again and I explained that I had already had an initial interview with them but I kept getting emails to schedule an interview. I told the receptionist that I thought maybe I should try it again. She explained to me that if they were going to offer me further interviews they would have contacted me by now. It had been about three to four weeks since my initial interviews. She took my name and number and said she would check and call me back.

She did not call me back that day or the following day. The next day I decided to respond to one of the emails I had received for the regional manager that spoke at the information session. I explained the order of events as I had explained to the receptionist adding that I had spoken to the receptionist and she said she would get back to me and hadn't. I told him good luck seeking candidates to fill their positions. I then opted out to receive emails from them. I figured it made more sense to opt out then to keep getting them knowing that it did not mean to call again for an interview.

The crazy thing is that even with what I knew I still wanted to work there, for the money. I also reasoned with myself that I could be the change that they needed and that maybe God showed the truth about their company because he wanted me to be aware so I would not get caught up in it. The real truth is that I really did not want to work with such a company but I wanted to make that money. It seems that what they were operating in was trying to operate in me. After I sent the email to the regional manager and opted out of their mailing list I let it go and I am so glad that I did.

A little while after that I learned of a job fair being held at a hotel. I made plans to go. I had been hoping to hear about a job fair that I could attend and there it was. I continued to fill out applications and send my resume to companies. I did job searches on several job sites. I believed that I would definitely have something worthwhile after all the jobs I had applied to and after going to the job fair and applying to companies there.

I went to the job fair and there were a lot of companies there. There were quite a few companies there that were social service organizations. That was an area that I was familiar with and I was willing to check out opportunities in those companies but I was trying to stay away from working as a home care worker. I was willing to consider office jobs but they wanted you to have so much experience and I fell short there. I still applied to several of the companies and just utilized what had to demonstrate my ability to perform the jobs that were posted.

I was more interested in a sales jobs and I actually spoke to two representatives from a job that required sales. I told them that I was very interested in selling. They scheduled me for an interview to come in the following week. I gathered a lot of information from many of the booths at the job fair and sorted it all out at home. I actually applied with quite a few companies. The day of my interview I actually could not find the place. I had directions that the representative from the company sent me, and I got the directions from Mapquest. I noticed that the directions were not the same.

I initially set out to use the directions from the company but I got confused about part of the directions. Their directions said to follow a certain exit at the clover leaf and I was unsure what that meant at the time so I looked at the Mapquest directions and followed them. I could not find the address because it was not there. I then realized what the directions from the company meant by following that exit at the clover leaf so I tried to find my way back around to the expressway to take the correct exit to no avail.

It was getting closer to my appointment time and I did not want to be late. I called the telephone number that I had for them and only got voicemails. As I rode around trying to find my way back to where I exited, I noticed the entry on the expressway to get me back home so I decided to take it and go home. My attitude was that I tried my best to make it and that was all I could do. I figured that maybe it was not meant for me to work there, although I had a good feeling that I would do well on the interview and whatever else I had to do and that the job was mines if I wanted it.

On my way home I remembered that the lady I spoke to at the interview gave me her card and I decided that I would call her when I got home to let her know the situation. Either way I was going to email her and say something because that was the appropriate way to handle business regardless of what happened. When I got home I located the business card and called the number. I left a message explaining what had happened and I apologized for any inconvenience. I did not feel a need to ask for another appointment but I did indicate that she could call me back and I left my telephone number.

CHAPTER 39

In some ways I was kind of trying to get out of it and reasoned with myself that this job was not for me although I knew that it was mines if I wanted it. I did have this feeling that they were going to call me and they did. I say they because I believe that I spoke to someone different from who I left the message with. I assumed that they had different people that handled different duties and they would direct the information to whoever handled those things. Let me explain that better. When I went to the job fair, I spoke to one lady and very briefly to another lady that was there with her to represent their company. I was scheduled to interview with a different person. When I called and left the message with the lady who gave me her card at the job fair, she gave the interview information to the person or persons that scheduled the interviews.

The lady that called me asked if I could schedule another interview and I agreed to. She asked me if I could come in that afternoon or evening and I told her that I could only come in the morning. I could not come in that afternoon or evening or any for that matter because I had to be home to get Freedom off of her school bus and tend to her when she got out of school. They did not have any morning slots that week so she scheduled me for a morning interview the next week. She made sure that I was clear about the correct directions to their offices and I told her that I was and explained where I think I went wrong, pointing out that sometimes Mapquest gives the wrong directions. She agreed.

The day of the interview was right after a snow storm that took place over the weekend. That Monday I pressed to get to the interview. I thought Freedoms school bus would be late for sure after all the snow that fell the night before, so I asked Abraham to see to Freedom getting on her school bus so that I could get to the interview on time. Abraham agreed and I was off to the interview. I had the thoughts and belief that the interviewer or interviewers would see excellence in me and would realize that I am the perfect candidate for the position.

The position was for a sales associate in a call center. The man who interviewed me said that he was surprised that someone with my level of education would be interested in this job. I explained to him that because I lack experience in the workforce in the areas of my Degrees, I had to come in a company a little under my educational level but I know that I could work my way up. I believe that he thought of me as someone long term in the company that could actually help build and improve the company. The interview went really well and he did see excellence in me and felt that I was a perfect candidate for the position.

After the interview he set me up on a telephone line, gave me a script and had me to role play a call with him. After the call he came over to me and asked me how did I feel that I did. I told him that I noticed that I was trying to be conscious of not having the customer on the call too long and so I was talking too fast but I recognized it and talked at a slower pace. He gave me a very curious look and said that I did really good. He took me over to a desk where he handed my resume to a lady and asked her to email the simulation tests to me. He informed me that I would receive an email from the company to take a test that afternoon and that he would get back to me the following day.

I took the test and did really well. The interviewer called me back the next morning and indicated that he would like for me to come in for a panel interview. After scheduling the interview for the next day, I was having second guesses about the whole ordeal. In the meantime, I continued to search for day care providers for my daughter. That evening I went to see a day care provider and I was not at all comfortable with what I experienced. I tried to reason with myself that it was okay, not a big deal but I knew that it was not okay.

The lady had a dog that got all in Freedom's face when we walked in. She said that he greets the kids like that every day. Freedom was cautious at first but did not seem to be fearful of the dog. She got over it real quick and tried to get to where the toys were. There were other things that did not sit right with me. The whole thing just did not seem okay. I had checked with other day cares in the area that were open in the evening and weekend but they did not have any openings. I thought that I had to choose a day care that was in the area for the bus company to service her.

The next morning I called the interviewer and left a message that I would not be coming to the interview and I would have to decline from the job because of child care issues. The truth is that at the time there was a lot going on where I was trying to get away from my husband and Freedom was giving me a hard time too, so I was trying to get away from her too! The position had several shifts in which only afternoon to evening shifts were available and I would have to work one day of the weekend, either Saturday or Sunday. Again, because I was just ready to get away from my husband and my daughter and produce, I was willing to attempt working the inconvenient schedule. Attempt the schedule is exactly what I did because I realized that I would not be able to do it.

Once I came to my senses I knew that taking the job meant that Freedom would be out late, past her present bedtime and that would probably throw her off of her schedule and cause some problems. I did not want to use her PCA services for this because I would still have to pay out of pocket and the positions compensation wasn't enough for me to be making such a move. The interviewer called me back and told me that I did a good job on the simulation and he said that he would like for me to come in for the panel interview with several people.

I thought those were too many hoops for me to have to jump through for that job. I felt that some people may have to do that but

I felt that I was selling myself short when I didn't have to. If I was going to do interviews with multiple people, it would have to be for a better position and more compensation. I explained the day care situation and he asked me if a day schedule like nine to five or eight to four would work for me. I said yes and he told me that he would see if they could accommodate me and call me back.

After that telephone call I felt really bad about going along with the man instead of just telling him flat out that I no longer wanted the position. He was really good to me. He was very pleased with my presence, personality and performance thus far. I had won him over and he was going out of his way to ensure that I got a position with the company. I was unsure about what to say to him if he called me back. This may sound crazy but the good thing is that he didn't call me back and I did not call him back either. What I should have done is told him that I really appreciate the time that he took to interview me and I initially thought this job would work out for me but I realized that that was not quite the job for me.

See it was not just the small amount of compensation for my worth but the office was quite a ways from my house and I did not like the idea of working a weekend day. As I've already said I was willing to try it because I was ready to not only get away from my husband and my daughter but produce too. Eventually, I received an email from the company indicating that they had decided to proceed with other candidates. The truth is that I had decided that I did not want the position and they followed suit. In fact, the interview never called me back and said anything. I believe my energy said that I did not want the job and so things worked that way.

Going through these experiences ultimately taught me that I was ready to win. I had made such an impression on all of the interviewers, except on the company that was driven by greed (and I actually did there too) that I know that I could do the same thing when a more appropriate opportunity presented itself to me. I summed up the whole job seeking and interviewing experience with "it was practice and it showed me what I am capable of". I was full of confidence and so sure of myself and I exuded just that. I knew then that I could properly present myself in any other circumstance when needed.

Although I took on the perspective that I was practicing, I felt a little bad about wasting their time. I was sincere about getting the positions but I had no intentions on staying around too long and so I felt that I was giving them false expectations about me and that was not okay. I decided to take a step back and regroup. It was near the Christmas holiday and so I took a break from the job searching and decided that I would start fresh in the new year. I had definitely come to the realization that I did not want a nine to five job unless it was a lucrative salary and it had to be Monday through Friday with day time hours. I needed to be with my daughter in the evening and on the weekends. I had to be there for her.

CHAPTER 40

I had made a decision to apply with an insurance agency in the new year when I would have some money available to pay for training and licensing. Before the new year even came in, it was on me to work on my business plan for the special needs day care center. I made plans to start on that in the beginning of the new year. I began to focus my attention on preparing for the Christmas holiday and making sure I got my children and husbands gifts in time. I had to get Rasheeds's gifts in time to be sent to him so he would have them for Christmas. Abrahams birthday was also a few days before Christmas and so as always, I had to get enough gifts for him not only for Christmas but for his birthday too. All this had to be done within a specific budget, which I was absolutely grateful for.

Abraham took some of the load off of me for getting gifts. He got a couple of things for Freedom that I wanted to get her and he got a couple of things for Rasheed. One item which he wanted and another that Abraham thought he would like and I agreed. Abraham also gave me some money to help with my Christmas shopping. See, before Christmas, I was initially considering using the money that I had to pay for the training and licensing cost to become an insurance agent. After starting with the one company and having to withdraw from it, I realized time was passing. The company that I withdrew from had training options that were more reasonable than the first company I had considered. It could have all worked out had it been a more feasible circumstance for me but as I found out in little time, it was not.

After withdrawing from there and not being selected with the other company I realized that it was getting closer to Christmas and since I was not in a position making money already, I needed to use what funds I had for Christmas shopping. Then when the other hourly sales position that I initially interviewed for came up, that process was happening the month of Christmas. The job fair was on November 29th. The point is that once it was closer to Christmas and I had not started making money, I had no choice but to wait until after Christmas if I wanted to be an insurance agent.

After the holidays I started preparing myself to work on the business plan. Abraham had been on vacation from work and Freedom had been on vacation from school. I decided to wait for them to go back to work and school so that I could work better. I checked out a couple of books about starting and operating a day care center and I checked out some books about how to write business plans. Once I had the outline for a business plan in front of me I decided that it was best for me to read the books on starting and operating a child care center, take notes and then write the business plan.

Abraham had started getting more involved with the union that represented him at his workplace. Another man at his workplace had been the union steward for his work site for quite some time but the employers did not like how he was handling himself as an employee. He was causing more problems for all the employees rather than being a good example and he did not keep the employees at the worksite informed on what was happening with the union. Eventually there was a big argument between all of the employees and the young man and the employees wanted to vote him out and Abraham decided that he would step in.

Abraham started to communicate with the union representative that was assigned to his workplace. He started going to meetings and became really involved. There would be days where he would not go to his workplace on workdays and instead he went to work with the union. The union could pull him from work for that purpose and pay his wages. Some days he would go to work with the union during the day and leave in time to get to work for his shift that evening. He even attended some meetings and conventions on Saturdays.

A whole new world was opening up to him. He was able to see what the union was really about and how they operated. It was an exciting time for Abraham. The union leaders liked him so much that they decided to bring him on the team for two months. Initially he was told that they wanted to bring him on but it was not it the budget. Later they told him that they could pay him a salary of what he was already making. The only thing was that there would be some short work days and some long work days.

This new schedule was a big adjustment for us. I actually liked the fact that he was getting up in the morning and leaving out to go to work. It seemed as if it was the natural way of working. In other words, work during the day and sleep at night. The only thing about that was that he still had his second job to do in the late night three days a week. He worked that out and made it work.

Initially Abraham would complain about how unorganized the union was and how they lacked clear communication skills and to be honest I really didn't want to hear about it especially after hearing it so many times already. I eventually told him that he knew how they were going in and that is how they are and complaining to me does not fix the problem. He also would come to me for help and advice. One day he came and sat in the kitchen near me while I was in the front room. I could sense that he either wanted something from me or what he was doing on his laptop and writing on paper had something to do with me. I asked him was he getting ready to give me something and he said no.

Earlier that day I had called him and left him several messages on his telephone. I had expressed how I was unhappy about some events that had taken place that involved his niece, Sonya. I indicated that I had enough and would not be able to continue with the relationship any longer. I explained that I felt that he was taking my kindness for weakness and that it seemed that this would never change. What it all came to was that I was not going to continue in such a relationship. I mentioned this to say that after I left those messages, I am sure that he was not sure how to approach what he did next.

When I got up and went in the kitchen, Abraham said my name as if he was calling me or wanted my attention. I looked at him and he asked me if I could type something for him. I told him I was going to have to charge him. I told him it would be five dollars per page and I asked him how many pages he had. He rambled with the paper and I noticed two sheets of paper filled with writing. I then told him I could give him a discount and do both for five dollars.

I typed the document for him and I did not charge him for it. I was saying that to make a point that my services are not for free. I was in a place where I could not be giving free services to him all the time. Typing is a skill that I had developed and a very valuable one at that. Abraham was used to me doing so much for him that I think that he started to just take me for granted. I was at a point where I felt like I was being used and not properly compensated. It's not that I wanted him to pay me for all the things that I did but I did not want to be taken advantage of either.

Abraham indicated that what I had typed was a speech that he had to do the next day for work with the union. He asked me how do you do a speech and I shared some great tips with him. The next day he called me from the event and told me that he did his speech and he did really good and got a standing ovation. He said that he was really nervous before he gave the speech, while he was giving the speech, and he was still nervous while he was speaking to me on the telephone. He also said that the President of the union wanted to speak with him in his office and when he went to see him, he congratulated him and told him that he did a great job.

I was really happy for him. I told him that doors of opportunity were going to be opening up for him. I also explained that the key was in recognizing that it is God working through him and to allow God to do just that. He stated that before it was his turn to speak he asked God to help him and clearly he did. A whole new world was opening up to Abraham and that was really good for him. Abraham had been on the same job since he had come to America twelve years ago and started working. He also worked with his brother who worked as a contracted cleaning service. Abraham was actually feeling stagnant and I'm sure getting pretty bored with his work but he did it because he's responsible like that. That's one of the traits that I love about him. Also, I believe he was inspired watching me complete two degree programs.

When I met Abraham I was already working on my Masters Degree and he was there when I completed it and when I received my Doctorates Degree. While I was working on my Doctorates Degree he signed up for GED classes and went faithfully. He took the test a couple of times and had a hard time passing the reading part. Abraham's first language is French and although he spoke English pretty good he said it was challenging to read and comprehend the English language as fluently as he could in French. This was completely understandable. He stated that there was an option to take the test in French but he said that he wanted to be able to do well in English because English is the American language. He said he wanted to improve in his English dialect and reading comprehension.

Now Abraham speaks the English language very well. Sometimes he would use the wrong words for what he was trying to say or use inappropriate sentence structure. Many times I noticed that he listened to me intensely when I talked to him and I realized that he was learning the language from me. I would also use certain words that I believe he was unfamiliar with but sometimes he was able to figure out the meaning of the words by the way I used them in the sentences.

Abraham waited a whole year before he went and took the GED test again. The facilitator at the test center gave him some helpful tips as to what test to take to help him get the points he needed to pass the GED test. Abraham followed his suggestion and a few days later he received a call from the testing center indicating that he had passed the test. He was so happy and I was happy for him. That was a really huge accomplishment for him. Abraham was inspired and wanted to go to college. He was not a citizen or resident of the United States and could not get financial assistance to go to school. He felt that his personal finances at that time were not enough to allow him to pay for it himself. I am sure that as our finances increase, he will eventually be well able to pay for college. I am looking forward to that just as much as he is!

CHAPTER 41

When I was doing my job search and interviewing, I would talk to Abraham about my experiences. I spoke about how I wouldn't mind having a job where I had to travel as long as I had someone in place to care for Freedom. I believe Abraham started desiring something more for himself the more I shared experiences and spoke of other possibilities. I believe that that was how he ended up working with the union. He desired something different and meaningful and he attracted it to himself. The president of the union mentioned to him that there would be opportunities for him to travel to other states and they paid all of the expenses. I believe that when I talked about being open to a job where I could travel, he was motivated and desired a job where he could travel. After a couple of months of working with the union Abraham went back to his regular job and things went back to normal or somewhat normal, and that came with its challenges too!

I had come to a place in my life where I became observant and aware of how we as people attracted the things that we experience into our lives. That is what we perceive as the good and the bad. I came to understand that those things that were not so pleasant were there to teach me something. I like to say that everything in life is a lesson or a blessing and the lessons learned can be a blessing. That's if you get the lesson, meaning whatever the event came to teach you. I am not saying that it has been easy but I can say that God has given me so much grace to do the things that I am purposed to do. I've heard that God has a purpose for our lives and I absolutely know that it is true. In my life's journey I realize that Gods ultimate purpose for all of our lives is for us to get back to him. Remember who we are in him and let him be the ruling factor in our lives.

With that being said, I believe that it is up to us as individuals to decide what we should do as far as a career, education or any other things we choose do in life. Now I do believe that we should do the things that we feel led to do or are passionate about, skilled or talented in. These attributes can be indicators as to the direction we should take. Overall, I believe God wants us to be whatever we choose to be as long as we are honoring him. We just want to be sure that we are happy in what we choose and that we ultimately utilize the gifts God has given us for the highest good.

The issue with me is that I feel that I can do so many things. So many things are of interest to me. I had to work at taking it one step at a time and determining where my greatest passion was at the time, and start there. Although I did this, I often became attracted to other things that presented themselves to me. The key was to stay focused on what I was working on. Sometimes the things that I became attracted to were also indicators of other things that I could do at some point. The key for me was to recognize that for what it was and my ability to do that did not come easy. There was a lot of trial and error but the trial and error led me to getting the messages and directions that were revealing themselves to me. Yes, I felt like I was being pulled to and fro at first but once I learned to quiet myself, stay focused and allow Gods spirit to guide me, that dissipated. I continued to get better at this and eventually things started to come together.

Abraham and I are doing a lot better. That does not mean that we do not continue to have challenges but I must say that we are doing a lot better with the way we handle things. I still find myself doing a bit much where our relationship is concerned and I have my venting and tripping moments but they don't last and I am even getting better with that. One of the greatest things that I have learned is that I am equipped to handle the challenges that I have.

I also am mindful of the fact that Abraham is doing the best that he can. I see how he tries and I don't want to diminish the fact that he does try.

Yes, I have felt that the way that he goes about doing certain things is not the best way, but I've also realized that he has to find his own way. Furthermore, it is not my place to say what way he should go and how he should do it. I've had to learn to keep my opinions to myself and eventually I learned to not even have an opinion concerning the way he chooses. I must say that it was sometimes hard for me to watch him go about things in ways that I knew were not the best, knowing that it would not give the best results. But again, I had to let him figure it out and find his own way and just assist him where I could either when I felt led to do so or if he asked for my opinion, advice, or help.

Christina and I are still distant from one another although we both have made attempts to reunite. Sometimes other things have gotten in the way of that but that's okay. I love her and wish her all the best. I believe that it will work itself out on its own when we are both at a certain place and right now I can't say for sure where that place is. I do recognize that she has a lot of growing to do before it happens and while that's taking place I'll continue to grow too so that I will be in a better place, ready to receive her when that time comes.

Rasheed is still with his dad. He is doing well. He was not performing up to part during his sophomore year. His grades were slipping and he was not being as responsible as he could be. I had to get a little firmer with him and let him know that just because I was nice to him and we had cool fun times together did not mean that he could do whatever he wanted to and I would go along with it and continue to get him nice things. I told him that I don't take care of bums and that his only job right now was to go to school and do well. I told him that the way he was headed, was to be a bum.

I had not gotten him any new clothes, shoes, or anything else since I learned that he was not doing well in school and he was wondering when I was going to send him something. I eventually told him that I didn't have anything for him with those kinds of grades. I let him know that as long as he had clothes and shoes that fit he was fine. I was not trying to have him all decked out and he did not have good grades. He got the point and the next time I spoke to him he told me how much better he was doing in school.

I learned with Christina and Rasheed that you have to be careful not to give your children too much. It's important that they learn responsibility in the adolescent to teenage years to help better prepare them for adulthood. I did my best with Christina and Rasheed and I will continue to deal with them in a way that serves the higher purpose as best as I can. Sometimes that means not giving them what they want and being the bad guy in their eyes. Oh, and yes I am okay with that!

Freedom is doing very well. She has been making so much progress. She is communicating in such a mature way for her and she is learning how to better control her behavior. Freedom often has power struggles with me, particularly in the morning when I am brushing her teeth. Freedom has always been resistant to getting her teeth brushed and that is still a challenge. She tends to be difficult and combative at that time and although I know she does not like getting her teeth brushed because of her sensory issues, I am very adamant about brushing her teeth (and tongue) every day without fail. I do not want Freedom growing up thinking that it's okay to not brush her teeth just because she doesn't want to. I want her to understand that she should brush her teeth everyday because it's a part of having good hygiene. If I instill that in her now, although the challenges exist, she will continue to brush her teeth daily without fail. That's what I'm hoping for anyway.

As for Abraham and I, we recently had a really big blow up. The good thing is that understanding of one another and unity came out of it. Abraham and I finally had a real conversation concerning how we have been feeling about one another and our relationship. Abraham finally opened up and talked to me about his feelings and I actually listened to him, heard him, and understood his feelings and position. Abraham had been feeling like we were so separate, having separate lives.

The thing is that it was true. When I would try to talk to Abraham in the past, he never wanted to talk, that is about our issues or things I felt needed to be discussed and worked out. After doing that for so long I felt alone in the relationship and decided to leave him alone for the most part and tend to myself. I worked on myself and really started to grow and develop spiritually, emotionally, mentally, and physically. While I was doing my own thing he felt left out and abandoned.

From where I stood, I was only giving him what he expressed that he wanted. Now, let me also say that I had some ways about myself that made it difficult for him to connect with me. The thing is that I was subconsciously protecting my heart. He felt like I kicked him out and from my perspective he had kicked me out first and I followed suit. The cool thing is that when it was all said and done we both saw ourselves and how we both contributed to the problem. The wonderful thing is that we both wanted to repair our marriage and make it work and that is what we are doing. I find it amazing how a really ugly blow up helped us to get to where we needed to be. I do not think that it was a coincidence at all. I believe that God orchestrated the events that led to the blow up, that led to us actually talking and working things out. Abraham and I are in a really good place right now and I am excited about where we are going.

This experience has helped me to better understand that getting married is not necessarily a fairy tale just because you're married but you can make it your fairly tale. To get to that fairly tale, you have to go through some rough and maybe even dark places and if you can overcome them and become better and united more than ever, you can get your fairy tale. As the saying goes, you had to go through it to get to it. Let me be clear about this fairy tale. It does not mean that everything will always be perfect and go your way. The key is both parties wanting the relationship because of the love they have for one another and doing their part to not only maintain the relationship but improve it. Love is the greatest key and will allow you to understand your partner and be honest with yourself about yourself and what you need to check. I am so grateful that Abraham and I love each other enough and value each other and our marriage enough to work at it.

CHAPTER 42

As for me, I am doing just fine. I have learned so much throughout the years. My life has been interesting and challenging and I am grateful to God for all that I have experienced. I have come to a place of loving all that is. I am still improving that attitude and I always will be. The only thing is that now I will be improving it calmly and peacefully. I choose to eliminate force and control towards others from my life. God is in control. I am in partnership with him but he has the ultimate control. I am a co creator with him but he is the Creator. He is the Great I am that I am and I am that he is.

All of this may sound great but let me tell you, it has been a constant and continuous effort of being aware of myself, what I am being and how it is in correspondence with who I choose to be or better yet who I know I really am. I am also a lot more conscious of the way that my behavior affects others. In fact, this awareness has been a motivating factor to helping me to be conscious of unloving or non productive behaviors and transforming them to more loving, healthier and positive behaviors which are in alignment with God and the true essence of who I am.

I am absolutely happy to say that I do not get bent out of shape about much anymore and when I do it does not last. I almost immediately and sometimes immediately become aware of myself and let it go. If it is something that's really a concern that I need to tend to or come to some sort of resolve about, I completely depend on God to ultimately show me the answers and solutions. Doing things this way has really made a difference in my life. My stress level has definitely gone down and I am more mentally and emotionally stable and healthy. Overall, I feel so much better about life itself and I feel a lot freer to work at the dreams and visions that God has imputed in me.

I have to mention the fact that I make a conscious effort to keep my mind and attention on positive things. I believe in being present and I do practice being present and am continuing to work at that but I also not only think about those great things that I am expecting to manifest in my life but I am also feeling the feelings of being in that life. In other words, although those things have not manifest in the physical realm yet, I know that they are already mine and it all belongs to me and so I am grateful for it all now as if it were here now. Many philosophers, teachers, and theorists who practice and share their knowledge on the affects of positive thinking and how to attract what you want, will tell you focusing on the things that you want brings it to you.

Believing that I am who God says I am or should I say knowing that I am who God says I am or who he made me to be, although it's still being worked out in me helps me to become that who God says I am and made me to be. I must say that I am in a great place. I truly believe that all of my experiences have been to prepare me and propel me for where I am going. I also believe that this will always be the case. I believe that as I move forward in life, everything that I go through and experience will assist me in moving into higher ground. I believe as long as I am in agreement with it, and allow my experiences to make me stronger wiser and better (thanks Marvin Sapp), that is just what the results will be.

As the saying goes believe you can and you can. Believe you can't and you can't. I choose to not only believe I can but I know I can and all that I've shared with you was the beginning phase of what I am capable of. I am now walking into the middle of being doing and having (thanks Donald Neale Walsh) all that is for me. I have just shared with you the beginning of my life. I am on my way to the middle and I can't wait to see the end. I encourage you to do the same and I look forward to sharing with you my journey as I walk through the middle and I hope you stick around to here the marvelous end. I want to hear about your marvelous end too! Go for it!